PORTFOLIOS
in the Classroom

Tools for Learning and Instruction

Beth Schipper

Joanne Rossi

Stenhouse Publishers
York, Maine

Stenhouse Publishers, 431 York Street, York, Maine 03909

Library of Congress Cataloging-in-Publication Data

Schipper, Beth, 1947–
    Portfolios in the classroom : tools for learning and instruction /
  Beth Schipper, Joanne Rossi.
      p.   cm.
    Includes bibliographical references (p.   ).
    ISBN 1-57110-060-1
    1. Portfolios in education—United States.   I. Rossi, Joanne,
  1943–   . II. Title.
  LB1029.P67S35   1997
  371.39—dc21   97-19440
                                              CIP

Interior design by Darci Mehall, Aureo Design
Typeset by Technologies 'N Typography

Manufactured in the United States of America on acid-free paper
01 00 99 98 97 9 8 7 6 5 4 3 2 1

To Karen, Andrea, Pann, Tina, Julie, Lori, Sue, Mary, Janet, Joan, and John who took risks to help us learn.

Yellow Batons
by Jane Medina

I gave you some
thin, yellow batons
last September.
I showed you how to wave them
so that music would escape from
their tips.
I had imagined
searing music
—music that splits one's soul from one's heart.
But when you waved them
it sounded more like a groan
—maybe even a grunt.

So in October,
we put the yellow sticks back in their boxes
and started singing
other people's music, instead.
We sang in November.
We sang in December.

(Yes, I'd ask you to
wave them around
in the air, at times.
And at times,
I almost heard
someone get close to sounding a note or two.
Once, there was a whole bar's worth.)

We sang more songs in January.

In February, I told you to take out your batons,
once more.
You cut up the air into little shreds.
What a cacophony!
I despaired.

But in March,
someone alone in a corner
conducted a little tune.
It sounded like so many other snatches
—perhaps it was trite.
But I bounded over to that little someone.

"Do it again!" I cried.

April came,
and so did your folk tunes,
your chorus,
a lullaby.

Now it's May,
almost June.
There have been no concertos,
no sonatas,
not even an etude.
But here on my wall
I've pinned up
some sweet, short melodies
that came from
the tips
of your yellow batons.

Jane, a former music teacher, teaches in a bilingual 3/4 classroom in the Orange Unified School District in California. She wrote this after seeing her students' writing portfolios in May.

Contents

Preface vii

Chapter 1 What Is a Portfolio? 1

Chapter 2 How Do We Lay the Groundwork
            for Portfolios? 8

Chapter 3 How Do We Collect Baseline Data? ... 26

Chapter 4 How Do Students Select Pieces for
            Their Portfolios? 40

Chapter 5 What Is Involved in Conferences? 58

Chapter 6 How Can We Celebrate Portfolios? 81

Appendix A 85

Appendix B 97

Bibliography 103

Preface

One of us is blonde and one brunette, one of us is tall and one short, but our com monalties outweigh such minor differences. Both of us taught third grade as beginning teachers and were frustrated by the same questions, namely, what to do with students who weren't learning to read and how to evaluate students beyond simply giving them a grade. These questions led us to graduate school. We became reading and learning specialists and worked at school sites, but the answers to our questions remained elusive. When we finally met in 1986, we were both diagnosticians in the field of language arts.

In 1982, Joan founded the Foster City Reading & Learning Institute. It serves a diverse population of students of all ages, many of whom do not fit into regular classes and fulfill their curriculum requirements at the Institute. By and large, these kids have a difficult time trusting teachers, yet they rely on these same teachers to tell them how they are doing. The Institute often represents their last chance to succeed: they are frustrated, they are unable to read or write well enough to do their assignments, and they have low self-esteem. Their classroom teachers often lose sight of their strengths because their deficits demand so much attention.

Beth joined the Institute after teaching overseas, in Saudi Arabia and in Rome, for eight years. Together, we did hundreds of diagnostic tests for students with learning problems and taught individuals and small groups at the Institute and in area schools. Over the years our views changed. We began to focus less on standardized methods of assessment and more on the information we derived from reading and writing conferences with students, daily dialogues and observations, miscue analysis, and writing folders. Introducing the portfolio was an obvious next step because it captured the essence of learning over time, it corroborated testing information, and it offered a better way of communicating what students could do and how they were progressing. We began using the portfolio approach with all our students and it became a larger component of our assessment.

We had both been doing staff development in language arts assessment and began teaching part time at San Francisco State University. At the time, language arts instruction in California was undergoing an upheaval, and assessment was a hot issue. We developed a seminar on alternative assessment that we took to teachers across the country.

In addition, Robert Tierney and his colleagues published *Portfolio Assessment in the Reading-Writing Classroom* about this time, and we devoured the findings of his research as well as that of Sheila Valencia, Bill Harp, and Grant Wiggins on the same topic. We were confirming many of their findings with our own students. The portfolio became a natural adjunct to the reading and writing assessments we were using.

In 1991, Beth moved to the Los Angeles area, where she continued collecting data and doing staff development with teachers on using portfolios, while Joan continued to do the same in the San Francisco area. We videotaped students, held student conferences, and learned from teachers. Our discoveries are set forth in the following chapters, which explore our work with teachers as researchers and the effect of portfolios in their classrooms.

CHAPTER ONE

What Is a Portfolio?

Why use portfolios?

We've written this book to show you how to begin the portfolio process in your classroom without changing curriculum, without adding a significant amount to your workload, and especially, without increasing your anxiety. Once you see, as we did, the enormous value of portfolios—not just to assessment but to your students' overall learning—you won't want to give them up. The comments we've heard from students over the years say it all:

"I never thought I knew so much."
"I learned what I learned."
"I had no idea how much stuff I had learned about writing."
"My parents were finally interested in what I was doing."

What are the benefits of portfolios?

Photographers, artists, architects, dress designers, and those in similar professions have long kept representative work in portfolios, but they are latecomers to the classroom. Now that educators have begun to investigate the portfolio approach, teachers in almost every school district are experimenting with some aspect of portfolio development. Although the research has identified varying definitions of portfolios and their purpose, the findings reveal some common threads that are surprising and very positive. In the beginning, the focus of portfolio research was the product, the portfolio itself: What should it look like? How would it be scored? Where would it be stored? Who would read it? But to the surprise of many, the real value of the portfolio was the development *process*. The final product was far less important than the changes that took place in how students thought about their learning.

The strategic impact of the portfolio process is the self-awareness that is activated when kids generate their own selection criteria, make decisions, reflect on their work, and describe or name what they have learned. Discussing what they want to include in their portfolio and why, and analyzing which piece of writing or project meets those criteria create connections to learning far beyond the scope of traditional forms of assessment.

Finding time for something this important is not the chore you may think it is. Dropping one period of reading/writing per week and allowing students this time to make portfolio selections can accomplish a great deal.

They draw on their reading strategies in selecting important ideas.
They practice analytical and critical thinking.
They must evaluate, synthesize, and summarize.

This is reading and writing for authentic purposes.

We recall the second-grade teacher who was reluctant to devote time to portfolios. She did not think the children would like them, nor did she see their value, but she tried them because of a district mandate. We videotaped her students making their first portfolio selections, and she took the video home to watch. Later, she told us that she had learned so much about individual students. One feisty kid named Billy, she noted, sat quietly reading everything in his portfolio. The teacher realized that she had completely misjudged his ability to read and had mistakenly lowered her expectations for him. Watching the video gave her a different perspective on Billy's ability to focus on his work, to read text, and be motivated to learn. She also admitted sheepishly that she never knew her second graders could have so much fun simply reading and writing.

The process of portfolio development has a tremendous impact on student behavior. Students begin to

take more responsibility for their learning
actively engage in the learning process
develop and express a new self-awareness and think about their own thinking
grow in confidence and self-esteem
set goals for future learning

When we saw that portfolios set these kinds of changes in motion, we couldn't help but get excited.

Portfolios are valuable for students but they also affect teaching in important ways. Teachers have told us that using portfolios in their classrooms has increased student learning, but they also report that it has

- improved their instruction by compelling them to be more explicit
- made them more reflective about both their students and the learning process
- enhanced their ability to do assessment
- made teaching more fun

These teachers observe a real transformation in their students.

What are portfolios for?

These encouraging results are based on the use of the portfolio for small-scale assessments in the classroom. This involves the students, teachers, and parents. In this book our emphasis is small-scale assessment—but the term "small-scale" can be misleading. Portfolios are powerful tools, whether used as the primary method or as only one facet of evaluation. We want to distinguish between classroom use of portfolios and the grand-scale assessment that provides accountability to state and local administrators. Geof Hewitt (1995), the director of portfolio research for the state of Vermont, defines as grand-scale "any assessment program that involves teachers from more than one school . . . but when more than one school is involved, the challenge of obtaining consistent assessments is the same challenge that faces districtwide, statewide and national assessment efforts" (p. 164).

Although Vermont has blazed the trail, using portfolios for grand-scale assessment is still under investigation in many districts and states. Vermont initiated research on portfolios in 1988, exploring writing portfolios in order to identify the strengths and weaknesses of writing programs in individual schools. Evaluation studies pointed out that, in general, there was "appreciable but inconsistent progress," and teachers remarked on a tangible alteration in instruction that was in line with teaching goals (Koretz 1994). The state of Kentucky has used portfolios for writing and mathematics since 1992. Over a three-year period researchers saw significant improvement in students' basic skills (The Primary Program 1995).

Portfolio use in grand-scale assessment, however, is still in the pilot stages, and until states work out the bugs in their implementation, the jury remains out. In addition, changing assessment methods takes time. According to Donald Graves, "We need to explore the many uses of portfolios for at least another five years and perhaps indefinitely. Without careful exploration, portfolio use is doomed to failure" (Graves and Sunstein 1992, p. 1). We know of school districts that introduced portfolios but, because they had not adequately laid the groundwork, scrapped them after a few years, returning to the drawing board to redefine and reexamine their potential applications. Clearly, if we do not take time to explore portfolios fully now, the large stakeholders will force us back into the old quantitative standardized tests. Here, staff development is crucial. As teachers at all levels discover the power of portfolios in classroom instruction and learning, then even if portfolios are not adopted by the majority of states and districts for grade-scale assessment, their value will be firmly established.

■■■▭ What is a portfolio?

All portfolios are not created equal. Although some define them as a work folder, others as a place for standardized test score sheets and other performance assessments, we include the following strategic components (adapted from Arter and Spandel 1992):

A portfolio is a purposeful collection of student work that exhibits processes, strategies, progress, achievement, and effort over time. Each entry in the portfolio includes a student self-assessment reflection that is based on specific criteria.

What is "a purposeful collection of student work"?

Students compile a personal portfolio to showcase examples of their learning in a given subject. According to the Paulsons (1991), each portfolio tells a story and each story is unique for each learner. This does not mean that the assessment of daily work assignments is left to the end of the grading period. Instead, day-to-day assessment continues as usual in order to give you feedback on your instructional effectiveness and on your students' learning. As an assessment tool the portfolio demonstrates learning over time. Instead of sending all work home as soon as it is checked or graded, some is selected for inclusion in the portfolios. This allows students, teachers, and parents to compare the student's learning at various points in the year and from one year to the next.

Daily reading or writing assignments, for example, give us information about a student's day-to-day progress in and out of class. Each daily assignment adds a component to the student's profile at the end of the grading period. Portfolios, in contrast, allow us to see the "big" picture. They serve as a record of a student's overall learning. Each time students read the samples of work that have accumulated over a six- or nine-week period, they seem to become more aware of their own development and their own progress. This is the uniquely empowering, confidence-building aspect of the portfolio, and we have seen it with students from first grade to college.

One day Beth was helping some first graders make their initial portfolio selections when Margie, the teacher's aide, began crowing with excitement. "Look how much more Dan can write now. Bobby, you couldn't do this in September!" Margie was exuberant over the children's development. If the truth be told, none of us expected such dramatic evidence, and the kids were just as amazed. They seemed energized by seeing evidence of their growth as writers, and the teacher reported that afterward they were much more motivated to write.

What kind of work "exhibits processes, strategies, progress, achievement, and effort"?

Traditionally we have valued final products showing achievement and mastery of content. Now we add a further dimension—the processes and strategies that show how a student learns. The following chart lists some examples:

What Was Learned	How It Was Learned
Final published book with pictures	Steps of the Writing Process brainstorming, clustering, webs drafts showing editing
Final history report	Pages from learning logs and concept cards
A book report	Pages from Reading Response Journal showing: written predictions of the story summary of each chapter
Answers to comprehension questions	Tape recording of reading and retelling of the story

The process list (right) shows the steps to the final product (left). Process work is messy, but it offers evidence of thinking as it evolves and of learning strategies such as journals, writing drafts, and other graphic organizers. Students learn to value more than their finished work or their final grade; they begin to understand how they learn.

Any assignment we do in the classroom may be included in the portfolio, provided that its purpose and the evaluation criteria have been shared with students or determined collaboratively.

What do we mean by a "self-assessment reflection"?

Teachers have kept folders of student work for years, but what makes the portfolio distinctly the student's and distinguishes it from a work folder is the assessment of work the students themselves have chosen.

Self-assessment and reflection are the heart and soul of the portfolio.

Annie, an eighth grader from Orange, California, recorded the following thoughts:

> As a writer, I use writing not only as a form of expression, but as a way of sifting my own meanings out of life. Like most people, I try to learn from my mistakes, but I'm not usually aware of my own resolutions until after they're written down. Instead of being able to revise the words I speak, I have to feel my way through paper to explain my thoughts. As a writer, I must be a rough draft first and an editor second in everything I do. This is how I bind the book that is so uniquely me.

An imaginative response like Annie's does not happen in a void. Her teacher has introduced portfolios in her classroom, and their effects are influencing the students' thinking.

What do we mean by "based on specific criteria"?

Students are better equipped to tell the story of their own learning when they participate in determining the criteria by which they will evaluate their work. Students unfamiliar with the assessment process may rely on the criteria they learned from their parents or through traditional grading practices. In the past, teachers rarely shared evaluation criteria with students, who were in the dark about specific qualities that might show writing development. We have said, "Susan, this is *good* work," without saying *why* it is good or in what particular ways it meets the assignment criteria for "good." "Teacher talk" with students needs to be much more specific.

- "Elana, this is the first time you have written a paragraph with a main idea and supported it with details. You may want to consider choosing this piece, which shows an important milestone in your writing, for your portfolio."
- "Tom, your responses to your book show that you asked some meaningful questions, a strategy effective readers often use."
- "Maria, your prereading activity shows that you are drawing on background knowledge to make predictions and improve your understanding of the text. Would you like to put this in your portfolio to show your parents?"

Statements like these name the specific criteria that can help students and teachers evaluate student work. Unless we make it a habit to discuss such criteria formally, in class or during conferences, how will students know what works and what doesn't? Arter and Spandel (1992) say it best: "How does the student know whether to be satisfied, ecstatic, or dismayed [about their work] . . . To the extent that criteria are shared, students are made a part of the evaluation and receive the power that goes with that specialized knowledge—power to recognize strong performance, power to identify problems in weak performance, and power to use criteria to change and improve performance" (p. 37).

What makes portfolios authentic?

Because they mirror classroom instruction and contain selections relevant to the student, portfolios are "authentic." The work chosen reveals the student's thinking strategies and writing process. Portfolios give parents a unique sense of what the teacher values and of how children participate in their own learning and assessment. Handing parents the portfolio to read before a parent-teacher conference is one way to show them clear evidence of their child's growth over time. In addition, the contents include multiple samples of a child's writing and responses to reading, which are far more informative than a standardized test score. But portfolios are also authentic for another reason. Each one tells the individual story of one particular learner. Portfolios do not lend themselves to being compared, ranked, or averaged. Students compete against their own record of achievement.

Summary

We now have a working definition of a portfolio, a definition that has evolved over the past few years. We have discussed the benefits of portfolios, and we have looked at the portfolio for small-scale assessments in the classroom and grand-scale assessment outside the classroom. We've also differentiated a work folder from a portfolio according to the specific criteria.

Next we need to demystify the process of assessment.

CHAPTER TWO

How Do We Lay the Groundwork for Portfolios?

What do we do first?

Papers spilled out of the work folders on students' desks. When we asked the kids in the class to select a piece of work for their portfolio, one they thought represented their "personal best"—something new they had tried, for example, or something that illustrated particular effort—they seemed puzzled. Later, when we asked them to comment on why they had chosen this particular piece, some did not know how to respond, while others wrote superficial remarks like:

"This was good, I got an *A.*"
"This paper was neat."
"I had good penmanship."

We felt frustrated. We had made a start by asking them to look over their work and think about it. Surely students should be able to make more meaningful comments; isn't that what the portfolio process is all about? But there was something missing. These students had never before been involved in assessing their own learning. They figured they were finished when they handed in an assignment to the teacher for a grade. Assessment was the teacher's job. (We heard from more than one student that they weren't being paid to assess their work but we were!)

It dawned on us that somehow, students had to be involved in assessment from the beginning. They had to be able to talk about their learning by naming it or describing it, and then reflecting on it. These key elements were missing from our instruction. That's when we realized that, although the language of learning and the language we use to assess learning were clear to us (we knew what *A* papers looked like, what *F* papers looked like), they were not clear to students. We had never shown them any examples. How were they supposed to know? We were guilty of what is commonly known as "assumptive teaching"!

What kinds of strategies demystify learning?

The eye-opening discovery that we had to lay the groundwork for portfolios long before the students actually began to compile them changed how we taught. As we reexamined our beliefs about assessment and instruction in reading and writing, we both struggled with a number of questions:

- What do I value when a child reads?
- What do I value when I look at a piece of writing?
- What kinds of work do I value in the content areas?
- How am I going to clarify the reasons for these value judgments and transfer this information to students?
- How am I going to name what I consider to be the characteristics of good comprehension?
- How will I introduce this discussion into my instruction?

We struggle with these questions every time we listen to students read and assess their comprehension, every time we evaluate a project, grade an essay question on a test, or pass a judgment on an assignment. We know when a student is reading for meaning, or when a paper deserves an *A*, but we do not always make this information explicit. It is a "teacher thing" that remains a mystery to kids.

If we do not articulate the specific characteristics of A *work, kids will have difficulty assessing what constitutes an* A.

We need to clarify these criteria in our own minds before we get to the assessment or evaluation stage—even before we begin our instruction—so that we can incorporate them into our instruction.

A reading example

If we value perfect word identification, then a student who makes numerous errors when reading is a "poor reader" and a student who makes no errors is a "good reader." But if we value comprehension, we withhold judgment until the student has retold the story. The student who makes no errors in word identification may not be able to retell the story in his or her own words, while the student who does make errors may be paying attention to whether the passage makes sense and correcting errors when it doesn't. The student's reading may be anything but fluent, but because he is making meaningful connections, his retelling will be more likely to give the main events in sequence, include important details, and require no prompts. The student who has made more errors in oral reading may in fact be the one with better comprehension.

A writing example

If we ask students to explain in writing why a book like *Make Way for Ducklings* or *Charlotte's Web* or *The Pearl* has become a "classic," we have to be clear in our own minds about the criteria we use to judge quality. These might include

- memorable characters that readers come to care about
- a special setting
- unique or memorable language
- special messages, such as morals
- a plot incorporating universal conflicts that have meaning for the reader's life
- hooks or gripping situations to keep the reader involved to the end
- story lines that have withstood the test of time
- recognition during and after authors' lifetime

Students need to be immersed in good literature over time, to talk about particular classics, and to be involved in regular discussions of the criteria that make these literary classics "good."

For many years we spent a whole semester in one middle school program discussing why a book might be considered a literary classic. By the end of the semester, students were able to differentiate between a classic novel and an ordinary novel. They even wrote to the authors, and the quality of their writing reflected their ability to stretch their thinking beyond "It was a good book." They became deeply engaged with the texts and began to see connections with their own lives. They were also better able to approach complex issues and acquired a richer appreciation for the power and beauty of language. Here is a sampling of their letters:

Dear Mr. Knowles,

I think your book *A Separate Peace* is wonderful. One question that came to mind when I read the book was how Gene and Finney could be best friends when Gene felt such anger, such envy toward Finney; and how he could perpetrate such an act of cruelness on Finney which was pushing Finney out of the tree.

To me, the emotional relationship between Gene and Finney is not the relationship two best friends should have.

When I say "emotional relationship" I mean that what Gene feels toward Finney is not the feeling that should exist between two best friends.

Sincerely,
Ricardo

Dear Jonathan Swift,

When I first went to buy a book for reading, I knew it would have to be good literature, but I never expected to like it. After reading the first twenty pages of *Gulliver's Travels,* I was attached to it. I read it religiously every night at nine. When I first got it I was wondering how I was going to use ideas to make this paper good, but the book was so creative it left me with a lot of ideas. The character Gulliver is the kind of person I want to be when I grow up.

It is amazing how you could take a step back from real life and catch all the faults committed by man, using horses and giants to explain how disgusting and cruel humans are. This has helped me analyze my life. It was exceptional how Gulliver adapted so well to his environment.

I wonder how you had these radical views before your time. At the end when Gulliver can't even stand his family, I wonder if Gulliver ever thought about suicide.

This is one of the most inspirational books I have ever read. It makes me want to discover other cultures and evaluate mine. I want to find wrongs in the world and change them to make them right.

Your dedicated reader,
Ben

Dear Alexander Dumas,

"All human wisdom is contained in the words 'wait and hope'"! This was the message which I learned through a book you wrote called *The Count of Monte Cristo.* This is a book that truly inspired me due to its irresistible appeal. It is filled with love, suspense, adventure and triumph between good and bad. I have often wondered what is good and what is bad. After reading this book I have understood it. From reading just this one book, you strike me as a talented writer with a vivid imagination.

I especially liked the language used in the book. It is well expressed and yet it is easy to understand despite some of the French words that are used in the book. Your choice of words seemed to fit perfectly with the contents of the book, like a jigsaw puzzle. As I read the book, I could clearly visualize the happenings of the book. I undoubtedly admire the style of your writings. Maybe some day, I can be a writer, too! To tell the truth, this is the only classical book that I truly enjoyed.

Sincerely yours,

Grace

Of course, discussing and naming are not enough; we need written criteria—but we're coming to that.

A content area example

In a typical fourth-grade science experiment involving green plants, students study what happens when they put one plant in the closet and the other on the window-sill. Both plants receive identical treatment (water, plant food, etc.). Students keep a record in their journals of their hypotheses, daily observations, any pictures, charts, and diagrams of plants, and their conclusions, which may or may not support their hypothesis. When it comes time to evaluate their journal entries, they might consider the following criteria:

- Have they used accurate descriptive words to tell what happens day-to-day?
- Have they offered a reasonable prediction about what will happen to both plants?
- Do their diagrams/charts accurately reflect what they were learning about plants?
- Have they reached a reasonable conclusion to explain what happened and why?

Daily discussions of the "scientific method"—the procedures scientists follow to reach their conclusions—will clarify the process. During the instruction about plants, for instance, the teacher should show students examples of journals that record accurate and complete observations and journals that do not. Figure 2.1 shows sample records kept by second graders, who were practicing their observational skills after talking about criteria for observing.

It is not enough to clarify the criteria for conducting a scientific experiment in our own heads, nor is it enough to discuss the issue during instruction. Even demonstration is not enough. The criteria for appropriate journal entries should be written down and displayed where children can see and use them.

How do we get students to name what they are learning?

In reading

Our struggle to define the criteria for good work in different areas was just the beginning. We also needed a way to make sure that what children learned stayed

Figure 2.1

Examples from Fourth Graders Practicing Their Observational Skills

BIG **Big plant** July 6, 1990 new leaf	July 6 1990 I gave plants ¾ of a cup of water with fertilizer in it. 5 drops
Balb 3 July 6, 1990 1"	
Balb 2 July 6, 1990 new sprout ¼ of a " tall	**Balb 1** July 6, 1990 Tring to sprout

Figure 2.1 Continued

Plant Observation

July 2, 1990

July 1990, 12 | July 3

Bulb three

Bulb three ¾ and 4/16 of a"

Bulb one

Bulb one no sprouts

11, new sprot ⅞ of a"

July 9
Bulb 3 is two"
tall. On the 9th has
grown to ½.
11 3" tall
12 has grown ½"

Bulb two

July 11 sprot ½" tall.
July 3 new bulb, sprout

Todle hight
of Bulb 3" and a
½ Bulb leves
are dividing and
a new sprout
is growing

plant 8" half green | July 3 — 11 leves on plant

9½" two new leves | The top part of plant

July 11 two new leves. Todle of leves
17. July 12 has grown 1 leve
todle of leves 18. On the 16 plantsleves
have gone.

Bulb 3 b6 is now 5" tall

Figure 2.1 Continued

Plant Observation   July 2, 1990

1. Dry
2. wet (if put water)
3. soil
4. green plants
5. Has some of the roots.
6. needs water
7. 4½ foot
8. 4½ inches
9. 11 centimeter

July 3, 1990

7½   How many leaves 2?

                                    July 6
1. It grew another plant   1 It grew another
                              plant. It got taller

July 11

    It is growing and we are putting
food for the plant. It got new leaves
too.
    It grew 1¾ inch   July 12, 1990
                       1. It grew 1 inch
        It has 28 leaves

with them. But asking them to recall what they learned yesterday is a poor way to reinforce learning. Students need to *experience* learning: to describe or name what they are learning and make it their own. Since reading instruction is our forte, we decided to focus on this area. Because reading, unlike writing, is an invisible mental process, we looked at the behaviors or strategies good readers use (Pearson et al. 1992). We talked about these strategies, modeled them, taught students how to use them, asked students to practice them, and helped students name or describe them.

Although this kind of strategy talk was not new to us, we had not previously acknowledged its importance by writing it down. By naming strategies for students, we give them ways to discuss what they are learning. We call this process "charting."

Charting is simple and straightforward; it involves naming and writing down on chart paper the important strategies, steps, or characteristics of a process to serve as a reminder of your instruction.

In reading the story of Cinderella, for example, the teacher has just asked the third graders to find a sentence that might tell why Cinderella's stepsisters were so mean to her. Many of the students find sentences, and the teacher asks Jessica to read hers. The text says, "The father loved his younger daughter more than anything else on earth." Jessica reads "The father loved his younger . . ." and stops. Phonics may be the only strategy Jessica has used up to this point, but *daughter* unfortunately is not phonetically regular. She needs another strategy. The other students are poised to supply the word, but the teacher steps in and tells the class to watch how Jessica figures it out for herself. He then asks her to try a word that does make sense. Jessica reads, "The father loved his younger son . . ." The teacher tells Jessica that although *son* makes sense in the sentence, the author has used a word that begins and ends with different letters. Can she come up with a word that still makes sense but begins and ends with those sounds? Jessica tries to sound out the word and says *daugger.* The teacher reads the sentence back to her and asks if that word makes sense to her. Jessica says no. Can she use what she already knows about Cinderella to decide whether she is her father's son? With luck, Jessica will move further in the direction of sense-making and come up with *daughter.* But if she doesn't, the teacher continues to coach her.

It would have taken less time to give Jessica the correct word, but that might not have encouraged her to be self-reliant or to try these successful strategies.

Instructional time is well spent when we ask students to name and apply a reading strategy they have practiced before.

What this kind of teaching demonstrates is that reading consists of more than correctly identifying words, or finishing a story, or picking up the surface detail. It emphasizes the more important purpose of reading, which is meaning making: bringing *meaning* to the sequences of letters, words, and sentences on the page.

The teacher asked the class what strategy Jessica had used to figure out the word when she got stuck. As the students described the process, he put their words down on chart paper under the heading What Effective Readers Do When They Get Stuck on a Word.

What Effective Readers Do When They Get Stuck on a Word

Skip over the word and read to the end of the sentence.
Go back and put in a word that makes sense—read the words around it or use picture clues.
Try a word that sounds like the way we talk.
Think of a word that begins with the sound of the first letter, ends with the sound of the last letter, and blend sounds for a real word.

Students copy this chart into their journals so they can refer back to it when they are studying on their own or with someone else. As a result of this experience, the teacher began to develop a set of similar charts during reading instruction.

Charting is also effective on the primary level, with emergent readers. In a small-group discussion of a book, our instruction might consist of

reading to students to help them develop a sense of story and story sequence
modeling the use of prediction in reading

With the children we practice making predictions about what will happen next, retell the story in sequence, write down the retellings, and then try some cloze passages with text we have already read or written together as a class. During each step of this shared book experience, we talk to the class about what we're doing. Afterward, students know how to compile a chart of their own:

When We Read Stories Together

We make predictions about what we are going to read.
We put in words that make sense.
We tell what happens in the beginning of the story, in the middle of the story, and at the end of the story.

Primary-level children tend to become good at naming the strategies, so this is not something that is beyond their ability. The following story is a case in point. An elementary school principal and part-time college professor of reading told us about a first-grade teacher in her school. One day when she stepped into the classroom she overheard a discussion between the teacher and the thirty squirming first graders sitting on the floor at her feet that stopped her in her tracks. The class had apparently just finished sharing a Big Book, and the teacher had asked the children how they thought they had done. According to the principal, these six-year-olds had begun discussing strategies in the kind of language used in her own graduate courses in reading instruction. She heard the students say, "We made predictions about the story, we told the main parts, and we put in words that made sense." She was amazed. "Of course!" she said, "Why do we keep this a secret? Children need to know why and how, and this first-grade teacher had definitely been calling attention to the strategies that good readers use."

For children at the upper levels, instruction in reading might focus on

- using prereading strategies such as previewing and predicting, asking questions, and drawing on background knowledge
- using different cue systems—syntactic (grammatical structure), semantic (sense-making), and grapho-phonemic (visual patterns and sounds of the letters)
- monitoring reading and self-correcting when text does not make sense

A reading chart for these children might look like this:

Strategies for Improving Our Comprehension

- Preview before we read by looking at the title and any vocabulary we might know.
- Predict what will happen.
- Use context clues to put in words that make sense when we get stuck on a word.
- Use the sounds of the letters to help decode the words we don't know.
- Correct ourselves when we read a word that does not make sense.

Because reading charts usually mirror the information emphasized in the teacher's instruction, charting can be a useful way to monitor instruction: if the goals and outcomes the teacher has emphasized are not reflected on the charts, the charts do not match the emphasis of instruction. That's important information. To connect with students, we know we need to change direction.

In writing

When children write every day, several times a day, and for different purposes, teachers can call their attention to the processes and strategies they encounter. The more students practice writing, the more at ease they will be in doing it. At that point, they can more easily reflect on which processes and strategies they are using.

By using the appropriate words (naming) for different aspects of the writing process, teachers demystify instruction. They let kids in on the essential terms they will use all their lives. When children first compose a story, they should know that this is a "first draft." As they begin to write more than one draft, teachers can introduce the terms "editing" or "revising." (Even if young children only add more text to a first draft in the revision stage, they are revising.) By becoming familiar with writing terms early in their schooling children will be able, with repeated exposure, to identify and name what they are doing.

Instructional components for primary-level beginning writers may include

- revising stories to elaborate on or explain certain parts to the reader
- correcting drafts using the conventions of English—capital letters at the beginning of sentences, periods at the end, spaces between words, correct spellings, and so on

A class chart based on these components might look like this:

How Writers Fix Their Writing

They read what they have written to someone else.
They answer questions about their writing.
When they make a mistake, they bracket it and change it.

The revision strategies students in this particular classroom learned are reflected in the class writing chart.

Instructional components for intermediate writers may include

- using attention-grabbing hooks and descriptive language
- revising and editing using read-alouds and conferences

A class chart based on this instruction might look like this:

How Writers Edit Their Writing

They do a lot of reading to see how other authors get their readers' attention.
They use description to paint a picture.
When they finish their first draft, they read it aloud to a partner.
They ask if their partner sees a hook at the beginning.
They put a mark on the paper next to sentences that are not clear to their partner.
They explain what they meant in those passages.
They revise their writing to sound like their explanation.

Defining and explaining the steps in the writing process require regular teacher modeling and regular student practice over time.

In content areas

As students accumulate experience in the content areas, they need the same kind of modeling and naming: if they are conducting experiments, for example, they need to know the procedures and the terms for these procedures. At the beginning of the school year, one teacher asks her fifth-grade class to draw a picture of what they think a scientist looks like. Most often she gets pictures of men in "nerdy glasses." But when she asks students to do it again at the end of the year, after they have gained hands-on experience in different areas of science and met some working scientists, their drawings are more likely to show a young marine biologist in a bathing suit conducting experiments on a boat. Their perceptions have changed because they have extended their learning. The following chart illustrates how their knowledge base has expanded:

What Scientists Do (September List)

- They experience new things.
- They do research.
- They are scientific.
- They try their best.

How Scientists Conduct Experiments (May List)

- They ask questions about why something happens.
- They set up materials to try to find an answer to their question.
- They form a hypothesis, which is a guess based on what they already know.
- They try things out to see if they work.
- They keep careful notes about what they observe.
- They study what happened in their experiment.
- They decide whether their hypothesis is right or wrong.

In addition, they have acquired more terminology to use in designating and describing what they have learned. If necessary, they can refer to the chart to refresh their memory.

▬▭ Why is charting so necessary?

Charting offers at least five advantages, all of which have a powerful effect on teacher instruction and student learning.

1. *Charts are measures of instructional effectiveness.* When students collaborate with the teacher on a chart, they volunteer their ideas about what they have just learned, whether it is a concept they need to know for a test or a strategy for studying more effectively. This information gives the teacher evidence of how they have interpreted the day's instruction. It serves as a mirror of the teacher's instructional effectiveness. Charting encourages ongoing teacher self-assessment.

When Beth was working with teachers-as-researchers on portfolios, one experience confirmed the importance of charting. Andrea Ambler, a junior high teacher, agreed to work with Beth because she too was developing portfolios in her classroom. She joined with other teachers from the same district to share portfolios and reflections. When Beth read students' self-assessments, she noticed that Andrea's students were more able to name their learning and evaluate their work in terms of the criteria for different types of writing. (We have used several samples from Andrea's classroom in this book.) Students in similar schools, in contrast, struggled fiercely when writing their self-assessment. Beth wanted to analyze what might explain the difference. She discovered one major difference when she listened to Andrea give instruction: During the instruction and practice periods, Andrea frequently named the type of writing. She also charted the criteria for each type in the homework assignment sheets; in her classroom, the walls were covered with charts reflecting her instruction. For reading and writing about autobiographical incidents, the description of characteristics and features looked like this:

Autobiographical Incident

About an important past personal experience and its significance

Characteristics:

    relates a specific occurrence in the writer's life
    uses a natural, honest voice
    contains vivid sensory details (showing instead of telling)
    contains self-disclosure

Features:

    captures the reader's interest from the beginning
    includes a setting and a sequence of events
    contains specific details to help the reader visualize what happens
    shares strong personal feelings
    explains a significant event in the author's life

In assessing their writing, students could refer to these charts for the specific characteristics and features Andrea had included in her instruction. Likewise, during peer conferences, the charts helped them critique each other's writing using the language of autobiographical writers. They knew the characteristics that distinguish autobiography from, for example, persuasive writing. When the state assessments for writing were given, her students scored consistently higher than students in most other districts. By clarifying and naming the criteria, Andrea encouraged their learning.

2. *Charting gives teachers diagnostic information.*   When students have difficulty in naming the strategy or concept they have just learned, teachers need to ask questions to discover where—or why—they lack understanding:

Do you have any idea why this is difficult?
Did you find it hard to concentrate?
Were there words you didn't understand?
Did I go too fast?
Are you worried about something?
Would it help if you drew a picture of this process?

Once when Joan was working with a fifth-grade class, the teacher allowed her to chart the important math concepts they had worked on during the previous few weeks. To her surprise, since her main emphasis had been problem-solving, the class chart instead reflected exactness in calculation. With this useful diagnostic information in hand, the teacher was able to go back to the drawing board to clarify and modify her instruction—and she certainly became more explicit in *naming* it.

By charting and asking questions, the teacher can determine where instruction and interaction may have broken down. Without this feedback, it is too easy to waste valuable time trying to move on while students become frustrated.

3. *Charts are valuable references during class.*   Sending the children to the appropriate chart when they are stuck, or have forgotten how to do something, is itself a strategy for building independent learners. The charts also save time, since they free the teacher from repeating information and remind students of past instruction. It does not take very many trips to the charts before students who are stuck begin to check them on their own. As a teacher we know recently noted in her journal: "I can't believe how much time charting saves me. I was always repeating everything for the students who did not listen. Now I just send them to the chart!"

4. *Charting is a technique that lays valuable groundwork for student involvement in the self-assessment process.*   When students use the charts, they are able to compare their work to the process outlined on the chart. In this way they take responsibility for their own learning.

5. *Charting provides teachers with a progressive record of their instruction.*   The charts serve as an accounting system for the content and strategies the teacher has covered, and the processes students have practiced. Charts are powerful tools during

parent-teacher conferences and during Individual Educational Planning sessions for students in alternative programs. Parents and administrators who question the validity of a student's progress—or lack of progress—can be invited to study the charts and review the student's performance in light of the instruction the student received. Charts are also powerful aids for a review of teacher performance.

What are some guidelines for successful charting?

There are no set rules for charting. The process, however, is best used sparingly, with new instruction or when the need arises in class. Resolving conflict, solving a story problem, doing research for reports, and managing one's time for homework are examples of the kind of charts that are most meaningful to learners. At the same time, the process should not be overused or it will lose its effectiveness.

Chart only the most important strategies and processes. Carefully list strategies that you value and those that are mandated by your district or curriculum. Whenever it is appropriate throughout the year, incorporate these strategies into instruction in different contexts and subject areas. For example, students can practice strategies for increasing comprehension such as locating an answer by skimming or scanning.

Set aside time so that students can copy the charts in a special section of their journal. Copying a chart may take only ten or fifteen minutes, even less in the upper grades. Students will gain a greater respect for the charts when they begin to use them for self-assessment, for example, in selecting work for their portfolio. Each time the class charts a new strategy or process, students can write it up in a mini-newsletter and bring it home. Parents have told us they find these strategies quite useful during the nightly program of homework, and they always add, "Why didn't someone tell us how to learn when we were in school?"

Vary the charts to keep students involved. In the beginning, the teacher will need to demonstrate the charting process, but once students understand how useful charts are in doing their work, they can create the charts themselves. Working in pairs or collaborative groups students can record ideas individually and then gather them together on a sheet of chart paper. The groups then try to reach a consensus as a class about which chart works best. The resulting discussion will provide the teacher with valuable assessment information. The process of charting should always be meaningful and fun, more like a game with enough variety to keep students' interest. In our own university classes we frequently assigned collaborative chart-making after we had covered new study skills. During their final portfolio conference, the students admitted that the process of generating the how-to charts really synthesized their learning about strategies.

Use charting for reviews during evaluation periods. Naming and charting learning strategies during instructional lessons gives students a real advantage. They need hardly ask what's going to be on the test. To prepare, they can refer to the charts or to their journals or learning logs, meeting in pairs or groups to answer relevant questions of their own devising. Preparing for tests and other assessments in this way may seem time-consuming, but involving students in their own assessment process actually saves time. It offers students one last opportunity to name and learn what has been addressed in class, before they are tested.

We need to help students succeed before we begin to evaluate them.

What else needs to be done to lay the groundwork for portfolios?

Strategy 1: Model assessment talk by identifying specific aspects of the student's learning

Specific comments offering positive assessment in the language of everyday instruction will avoid hours of review and even—surprisingly—save on time devoted to discipline. Naming what a student has accomplished confers dignity and respect on the effort, the thinking, and the learning. Indeed, when a teacher discusses test results, students can quickly distinguish between a facilitating and an intimidating tone.

Assessment can take two forms. The first offers collaboration and teamwork ("Doug, I can see this test gave you problems. Do you have any ideas about how we might change the approach next time we prepare for a test?"). The second stifles the desire to learn and diminishes the student ("Doug, I just don't understand why you did so poorly on this test! You could have done better!"). Discussing weaknesses in terms of "new areas to develop" or "goals to shoot for" enhances open, honest communication and gives the students a stake in wanting to improve.

If students are going to be involved in positive assessment, they need to hear the language of positive assessment every day. But few of us experienced such modeling during our own schooling. A good way to approach it is to point out "positives" in the student's current work and to *verbalize specifically* (this is very different from phrases like "Good work," which convey empty praise):

- "Look at this, Terri, you've begun to write whole sentences."
- "Susan, I noticed you stayed on the task today for five minutes."
- "Tom, I see three supporting details in that paragraph. Wow!"
- "I noticed you didn't stop reading when you came to a word you didn't know, Lori. You continued reading and then went back and put in a word that made sense."
- "I really liked how clearly you explained the equation in math class, Larry."

Making specific assessment conversation a habit when you interact with students is an important step toward reshaping your classroom environment according to the "asset model" of assessment. When you model positive statements, students begin to hear the "language" of assessment. When you name the specific strategies, concepts, or ideas that have been part of your instruction, students begin to understand what you value. If students hear about "neatness" and "correct answers," they will come to believe that in your classroom, learning consists only of neatness and exactness. But if they hear you talk about "taking responsibility," or "using the process of brainstorming and clustering for writing," or "discussing an opinion and supporting it with a well-developed argument," they will begin to value these dimensions of learning. Evaluations like "Good Work" or "Excellent!" or "You are not doing your best!" are less helpful to a student than a statement about the growth you are seeing.

Positive feedback saves hours of discipline.

For more on this topic we recommend Alfie Kohn's *Punished by Rewards: The Trouble with Gold Stars, Incentive Plans, A's, Praise, and Other Bribes* (1993) and *Beyond Discipline: From Compliance to Community* (1996).

Strategy 2: Fill in your own knowledge gaps

Most of us are products of the "just write" school of writing, which based grades on proper grammar, mechanics, and spelling. Many teachers report that they were never graded separately for content and never learned the criteria for different types of writing. We need to fill in these knowledge gaps as fast as possible by educating ourselves in those areas where we come up short. We might read professional books in areas where we lack background knowledge or enroll in workshops and classes at a college or university. When our instruction is informed, we can begin to demystify learning for students by clarifying the elements of excellent writing and making the evaluation process simpler. In the bibliography we have highlighted those books we consider especially helpful and reader friendly.

Summary

Portfolios are embedded in the curriculum. Talking about assessment is impossible without talking about instruction. As we prepare to teach any concept, lesson, or unit, we need to have a clear idea of our goals and objectives. If we are explicit during instruction, we will have students who can explain their growth and progress during assessment.

CHAPTER THREE

How Do We Collect Baseline Data?

What constitutes baseline data?

Because the work included in a portfolio represents a student's learning over time and provides evidence of its breadth, it is important to carry out an initial reading and writing assessment during the first and second months of the school year. This baseline information is the first component of the portfolio preparation process. *Baseline data* consist of any sample of work that demonstrates what students can do in a certain area when they arrive in the classroom. This information serves as a starting point from which we can measure a child's progress, just as we put a mark on the doorpost in order to measure a child's physical growth.

How do we collect baseline data in reading?

During September and October we give individual students a diagnostic reading performance test, which consists of a reading miscue analysis or running record (Clay 1993) and/or a listening assessment. For the reading assessment, we select passages from graded texts or from publisher-produced sources such as *The New Sucher-Allred Reading Placement Inventory* or the *Burns/Roe Informal Reading Inventory.* The student reads aloud a short, untitled passage and retells the story in his or her own words. Another useful resource is the district reading specialist, who may be able to suggest other materials on this order. We also ask the student questions to elicit evidence of various types of comprehension—making inferences, thinking critically, identifying the main events, and synthesizing the story by giving it a title. We sometimes ask questions about vocabulary or background knowledge to verify whether the student has indeed understood the text.

We record the entire process on audiotape, analyze the tape, and then discuss it with the student. With students who are not yet reading—young children in the primary grades, English-as-a-Second-Language students, or students with learning problems—we check comprehension by reading to them. This listening sample then serves as the baseline data.

In analyzing this information, we look for signs of the student's strengths as well as for strategies the student uses to understand the text, and record this information on the form. We also note problem areas and any strategies a student needs to learn. Although grade level is not the issue in this analysis, we do want to know whether students can handle the texts we will be using. Figure 3.1 shows a sample of a filled-out Reading and Listening Baseline Information sheet (a blank version appears as form A.1 in Appendix A). We generally use the key included in Figure 3.1 to fill in these forms, but we advise you to design your own marking system if that would be better suited to your needs. If you are not accustomed to analyzing reading data, a resource like *The Whole Language Evaluation Book,* edited by Ken Goodman, Yetta Goodman, and Wendy Hood, is an excellent guide.

The following day, the students have a chance to listen to their tapes for a performance evaluation.

This is the student's first opportunity to try self-evaluation.

We ask students to fill in a form (see A.2) containing open-ended questions intended to help them assess their reading before the conference with the teacher. When students listen to themselves read on the tape while following along in the text, they become aware of their own reading behaviors and are more prepared to discuss their evaluation with the teacher. Student and teacher share their findings with one another and launch their assessment partnership.

What does this conference sound like?

During this first conference of the year, the teacher's attitude is key to students' future success at self-assessment. We are careful not to focus on deficits or the student will clam up. Instead, we focus on the strengths and strategies already in place. We also look at the strategies needed if the student is to become an even more effective reader. The dialogue might sound like this:

Figure 3.1

Reading and Listening Baseline Information

Name *Thomaso*   **Date** *9/28/95*
Grade *3rd*   **Teacher** *Mrs. Brown*

Reading Section Level   *2.5*   Independent
                                   3.0   Instructional

Listening Level   *4.0*

Oral Reading Observations (Omit for Listening Selection)

✓-	fluent
+	knows some sight words
✓-	uses phonics
no	uses phonics exclusively
✓-	uses context clues
✓	uses repetition

Key:
+ = excellent
✓+ = very good
✓ = good
✓- = fair
- = poor

Retelling

+	main points
-	details
-	in sequence

Comprehension

+	main idea
-	details
ESL	vocabulary
✓-	inference
+	critical thinking

Strategies Observed

+	uses background knowledge
✓-	self-monitors and corrects
+	synthesizes information
✓-	makes meaningful substitutions

Strengths:
- *loves to read!*
- *seems to get main events*

Areas in need of work:
- *using context to self-monitor & correct*
- *vocabulary; continue work in English vocabulary development*

Student's goals:
- *"understand more words in English; read chapter books"*

Teacher's goals:
- *develop strategies for monitoring comprehension & self-correcting*
- *strengthen vocabulary and sequencing*

- ESL—English as a Second Language
- Non-English Proficiency
- Limited English Proficiency

TEACHER: Billy, I wanted you to read and retell the story on the tape recorder so we can have a record of your reading at the beginning of the year. Since I don't know much about you, I need to find out what strengths you already have and what strategies you still need to improve your reading. In January and June you will read on the tape again and then we can compare your progress in reading since the beginning of the year. It will be very exciting because you will be able to hear how much you have improved this year. Your parents will be also be able to listen to the tape and hear how much you've improved. Won't this be nifty?

BILLY: Yeah.

(The discussion turns to Billy's performance on the tape.)

TEACHER: What did you learn about your reading when you listened to yourself?

BILLY: I read lots of words wrong and I should read better.

TEACHER: I noticed that you had trouble with some words, but I saw you beginning to do some things that good readers do. Did you hear yourself stop when you read a word that didn't make sense?

BILLY: Yeah.

TEACHER: When you stopped to think about that word you indicated that your brain was listening to the story, and when you read a word that didn't make sense, you stopped to fix it. Did you know that good readers use that strategy? Poor readers would just keep on going and not pay attention to whether they are making sense or not. So let's mark that strategy on this form. What do you think, Billy? Did you correct yourself every time you got stuck?

BILLY: Not every time, 'cause sometimes I couldn't figure out the word.

TEACHER: So what were you doing to figure out the word? Could you hear yourself on the tape? You were whispering.

BILLY: Yeah! I was sounding it out.

TEACHER: Yes, you were! Good readers use this strategy, too. In fact, you did a beautiful job. You kept sounding and blending the sounds together until you recognized a word that made sense in the sentence. When you did that I said to myself, "Yay, for Billy! He uses sounds and context clues together!" Let's mark that on the form under strategies that you use. How do you think you did when you retold your story in your own words?

BILLY: Good. I only missed the part about the baton because I didn't get it.

TEACHER: I agree with you. You retold the story and covered all the main points in sequence. The baton part was difficult because if you've never seen that word in print, you may not know what to say when you retell that part of the story. Do you know what a baton is now?

BILLY: Yeah, it's that stick thing that runners give to each other when they race.

TEACHER: How did you figure that out?

BILLY: Well, it says that she won the race even after she dropped the baton. So, I figured that that must be the stick. I saw a relay race on TV once.

TEACHER: I'm really impressed, Billy. You just explained to me another strategy that good readers use. You used your background knowledge, things you already knew, to give meaning to the story. Let's mark that on the form also. Did you know you were using strategies that good readers use?

BILLY: No, I just do 'em, I guess.

TEACHER: Yes, you do. How did you do with the questions?

(They go on to discuss the different questions.)

TEACHER: Do you have some goals for reading? Let's put them down here on the form.

BILLY: *(Thinks and finally responds)* I want to read bigger words and chapter books, and um, remember more about the story after I read.

TEACHER: Those are excellent goals. I have some goals for you also. I wrote them here. Number 1, become more consistent in monitoring your sense-making. Number 2, develop your vocabulary. Number 3, by January, learn to enjoy reading more. Is there anything else you want to add?

BILLY: No, it looks good to me.

TEACHER: Thank you for helping me learn about you and your reading. I think you've got a good start.

(Billy smiles with pride and walks to his desk.)

Conferences like this one help to establish a classroom environment that invites students to participate in their own learning. During the conference the teacher asks questions to focus on the student's use of strategies while reading. This language may or may not be new to the student, but it will develop awareness and encourage students to monitor their own reading behaviors.

How do we collect baseline data in writing?

Most teachers are more familiar with collecting writing baseline data because students usually do a writing sample during the first few days of school. In the past, we collected and graded it, but we suggest instead that you treat it like the reading baseline data. We ask the student to write a story or a paragraph on something he or she knows a lot about. To determine which developmental writing skills the student has already mastered, we take the writing sample home and analyze it, then schedule a conference with the student, just as we do for the reading sample. Here again, we look for strengths over weaknesses. For example, Chris, a third grader, wrote the following sample. His former teacher allowed him to type it on the computer because he had such difficulty expressing himself using a pencil.

TREES ARE GID BECAUSE THEY GIV ASAJANT [OXYGEN] TO PEOPLE. SOM PEOPLE DOT BLEV IN TREES GIV ASJNET TO PEOPLE. SOMPEOPLE COT TREES DOWN. ANNAMLS LIVE IN TREES AND WIHN THE TREES GIT COT DOWN THE ANNAMLS HAF TO LIV AND GOT A NOW HOME BECAUSE THEY OLD HOME IS DESROED

Figure 3.2 shows the Writing Baseline Information Form we filled in for Chris. A blank version appears in Appendix A (see A.3).

The conference about this piece of writing might sound like this:

TEACHER: Chris, what do you think about your writing?

CHRIS: I don't like to write.

TEACHER: Why don't you like to write?

CHRIS: 'Cause it's hard to hold the pencil and I can't think of anything to say.

TEACHER: But you had some good ideas here and you've done some things that good writers do. Can you tell what they are?

CHRIS: *(Shrugs his shoulders)*

TEACHER: One thing good writers do is to write about subjects they know. You seem to know a lot about what happens when people cut down trees. Where did you learn about it?

CHRIS: I like to learn about things in science. I talked about this with my dad.

TEACHER: Oh, terrific! Let me show you something else you did that good writers do. I marked it on the sheet. *(Shows form)* You gave the reader some interesting information. It's like a small report. You had a main idea and you supported it with details. Look, I was able to mark many of these ideas under organization. You didn't just put the ideas in any order. You told what happens first, next, and last. This is a cause and effect paragraph. Did you know that?

CHRIS: No.

TEACHER: Well, now you know. Let's look at some other things you did. You had sentences with periods at the end, and you used some sounds to spell some words you had never spelled before, like *oxygen* and *destroyed*. I'm curious. Why did you use all capital letters?

CHRIS: 'Cause it's easier.

TEACHER: Hmmm. Oh, you mean you're not always sure when to use capital letters?

CHRIS: I suppose so.

TEACHER: Should we put down capitals as something we need to work on?

CHRIS: I guess.

TEACHER: You wrote a report instead of a story. Most kids wrote stories. Why do you think you did that?

Figure 3.2

Writing Baseline Information

Name __*Chris*__ Date __*10/12/92*__ Grade __*3rd*__
ESL _____ NEP _____ LEP _____ Teacher _____

Developmental Level _____ Drawing pictures
_____ ✓ _____ Emergent writing
_____ Standard writing

Writing Observations

____✓____ dictates text
_____ writes in first language
____✓____ writes with invented spelling
____✓____ writes complete thoughts
_____ uses detail and descriptive language
____✓____ writes complex sentences
_____ writes for different audiences

Key:	+ = excellent
	✓+ = very good
	✓ = good
	✓- = fair
	- = poor

Organization

_____ uses prewriting strategies
____✓____ states a main idea
____✓____ story has beginning, middle, and end
____✓____ writes three related thoughts
____✓____ details support the main idea
____✓____ details in sequence

Process/Passion

_____ takes initiative for writing
_____ responds to teacher's questions
____✓____ has unique style, voice
_____ views self as writer

Mechanics

____✓-____ uses punctuation correctly
____-____ uses capitalization correctly
____✓-____ uses standard grammar
____-____ uses standard spelling

Strengths:
- *background knowledge, sense of sentence, sequence, concept of cause and effect*

Areas in need of work:
- *prewriting strategies, mechanics (caps, spelling), editing/proofreading strategies*

Student's goals:
- *spell more words, get faster on the computer*

Teacher's goals:
- *become more comfortable with writing, acquire strategies for correcting spelling*

- ESL—English as a Second Language
- Non-English Proficiency
- Limited English Proficiency

CHRIS: 'Cause I hate to write stories. I only like to write about real things.

TEACHER: Oh, I see. What kinds of things would you like to be able to do in writing this year?

CHRIS: Maybe spell more words and get faster on the computer.

TEACHER: OK, we'll put that down. I'm going to add another couple of goals for you. I noticed you didn't do any brainstorming even though you practiced it last year in Mrs. Simmons's class.

CHRIS: I hate brainstorming. It takes too long. I just like to write sentences.

TEACHER: This year I'll show you some ways to make it easier for you. OK?

CHRIS: I guess.

TEACHER: The other thing I'd like to add is that you become more comfortable writing stories. Maybe you can use some information you know to write some interesting stories?

CHRIS: Maybe.

TEACHER: Even though you don't like writing, weren't you surprised you did so many things that good writers do?

CHRIS: Uh huh.

Because of his spelling difficulties, Chris's writing has received a lot of criticism. Few people can see past his spelling mistakes.

Once again, the baseline conference has two major aims. One is to create a student-teacher partnership that encourages the student to take an active part in the conference and to assume some control of the evaluation process. The teacher points out students' strengths as a basis for building the writing skills but without ignoring weak areas. These she addresses through lists of areas needing work or goals. The second aim is to help the students become aware of their own strengths and weaknesses in writing. Unless they have some awareness of these underlying elements, they regard their writing as simple as a series of isolated assignments. The baseline conference is the first step in giving students the language to consider and select portfolio pieces.

We found these conferences a little awkward at first, but using a checklist makes the process easier and helps keep the focus on naming the strengths first. We still reminisce about the reactions of some kids during these conferences, most of whom had never before heard or talked about their strengths. Not surprisingly, they couldn't wait to have another conference.

Assessments are drawn primarily from the Reading and Listening Baseline Information checklist and the Writing Baseline Information checklist completed in September. Although children will be familiar with their baseline strengths and needs because of their conference, they should keep their first reading and writing samples in their portfolio all year. Without these first reading and writing samples for comparison, students will not be able to see the extent of their growth or reflect on the significance of this new learning.

Some teachers keep the first samples in their own folders and hand them out before students write self-assessments. Others staple the first writing sample to the portfolio cover, where it is available for comparison each time students write a self-assessment. In addition, we staple a photocopy of the baseline checklists on the inside cover of the portfolio to remind students of their starting point.

What about baseline data in the content areas?

We've focused on the language arts, but that does not mean that the same process can't be used in the content areas. We aren't content area specialists, but we've worked successfully with many content area teachers who have adapted this process for their own subject. If the purpose of baseline data is to establish a starting point, what students know before instruction begins, the one thing these teachers had to decide was what baseline data would be most meaningful for their purposes.

Two math teachers looked at their curriculum for the year and decided what background knowledge and skills students needed in order to be successful in their classes. One gave students several word problems to solve and asked them not only to give the answers but also to tell, in writing, the process they used to solve the problems. He also checked their straight computational skills by giving them some problems in several different categories, such as fractions, decimals, percentages, and so on. The other teacher found a math placement test that matched the district's curriculum and the text she would be using. Both teachers gave a simple survey to check students'

- interest
- study habits
- attitude toward the subject
- amount of time spent on homework
- sense of competence in the subject area

Although the baseline measurements were different, both teachers gained information about students they could share with them. This information is the foundation for conferences and for the portfolio process.

Science and social studies teachers have told us that they need information about their students in the following areas:

- background knowledge of the subject area
- reading skills
- writing skills
- study skills
- attitude

During the first few weeks of school, one of the ways teachers have measured students' background knowledge is to ask them to write down what they know about certain topics in their journals or learning logs. Sometimes the responses are in narrative form and sometimes in the form of a semantic map or a brainstorming list. Teachers can get a sense of a student's ability to write coherent paragraphs from this activity. The following samples of journal entries from a fifth-grade class concern children's background knowledge on photosynthesis.

- "I think photosynthesis is a photo or picture and a thesis statement. I really have no clue what photosynthesis means."
- "I think photosifies is something to do with a computer. Something like holloghans. I saw a T.V. show that had this computer that can make hollergram. Or it could be like something to do with photos."
- "I think it is when you guess how a picture would look like."
- "I thing photosynthesis are pictures because the word photosynthesis has the word photo and synthesis is like someby studies about picture drawings of art or something like that."
- "I think a photosynthisi is a graph you did and experament like a copy of someting a graph is a brainstorming your thoughts."

Teachers can get a sense of students' reading ability and background knowledge by using an assessment strategy called *cloze* procedure. A cloze passage might looks like this:

Photosynthesis is a process by which green _____ make their own _____. They get water from the _____ using their _____. They use the _____ in their leaves and the _____ from the sun to make _____. As a result _____ is released into the air. If green _____ do not get _____ they die.

(Answers: plants, food, soil, roots, chlorophyll, light, food, oxygen, plants, light)

To generate a cloze passage,

1. Select short passages that reflect some of the main concepts you will be covering during the semester.

2. Delete key words or every word at certain regular intervals (every 6th or 8th word, for example). Teachers often use nonstick tape (3M makes Post-it tape) to mask the words before they run off copies.

3. Ask students to fill in the blanks with words that make sense to them, based on what they know. Do not give them a list of words from which to select.

4. Scan the passages to see whether students have a grasp of the concepts. Even

if students have not inserted the exact word, they may supply one that reflects some knowledge.

For information on study skills and attitude, teachers have used short student surveys or inventories similar to the one used by the math teachers.

Is it realistic to try to have conferences in content areas with 120 students? Ms. Murdock didn't think so, but she was determined to develop portfolios in her seventh-grade science class. We told her about the "have chair, will travel" version of conferences. Once she had collected her baseline data and analyzed it, she made notes about each student on a checklist. Then she assigned students a project that involved reading and writing at their desks. She moved from desk to desk with her chair, and had a five-minute conference with each student. Some conferences were longer or shorter depending on the student. She discussed the strengths and the needs of each student, and together they set some goals.

We should put in a word about Ms. Murdock's classroom management during these conferences. She set up the expectation that this was a sacred time between her and the student that was not to be interrupted unless someone was dying. She made sure the assignment she gave was engaging and that students were clear about what they needed to do. Once the conferences were under way, her students understood the power of discussing their individual strengths and needs. Students reported that they really liked setting goals together with the teacher. In fact, she overheard Ray tell his friend not to bother Ms. Murdock because this was really "bad" (translation—"cool").

Figure 3.3 shows a filled out example of the content area checklist. A blank form can be found in Appendix A (see A.4).

■■□ What will be the focus of the portfolio?

We have spent September and October getting to know our students: we have acquired baseline information about them, and we have observed them for almost two months. We have used the language of assessment in our classroom instruction, made charts for new instruction together, and used language from the charts in our conferences. The students meanwhile have been completing assignments. We want to begin to keep some of this work at school so that students have a cross-section to choose from for their portfolios. Since teachers tend to focus on the subject with which they feel most comfortable, we felt less overwhelmed in the beginning when we focused on just reading and writing and added new subjects gradually.

Before we go any further, we have to make a decision about the focus of the portfolio:

- Will it be only a writing portfolio?
- Will it have reading and writing assignments in it?

Figure 3.3

Content Area Baseline Information

Name _Ricardo_____ Date _____ Grade _6th_ Teacher _____
ESL_____ NEP_____ LEP_____ Content Area _Math_____

Observations

✓	study habits
✓	interest in subject
✓-	assignments completed
✓	participates in cooperative groups
✓-	works independently
-	participates in class discussions
-	can read text
✓-	has appropriate writing skills

Key:	+ = excellent
	✓+ = very good
	✓ = good
	✓- = fair
	- = poor

Skill Areas Needed for Competency (Here teachers list specific skills required for their subject area.)

✓	whole numbers
✓	decimals
✓	fractions
✓-	percentages

Problem-Solving/Thinking Skills/Concepts in Subject Area (Here teachers list specific concepts required for their subject area.)

✓	operations
-	measurement
✓	time
✓-	money
-	word problems

Strengths:
- strong computation skills; good grasp of concept of math and operations; works well in groups; hard worker; always attempts assignments

Areas in need of work:
- lack of English proficiency slows progress in certain areas such as word problems; needs help reading the book

Student's goals:
- get better at reading and writing

Teacher's goals:
- have Ricardo become familiar with key math terms and signal words in English

- ESL—English as a Second Language
- Non-English Proficiency
- Limited English Proficiency

- Will it have examples from content areas such as science, math, social studies?
- Will it also contain work from art, PE, music?
- Will it encompass a mini-portfolio in each subject area that is combined at the end of the year?

What goes into a work folder?

The last component of the portfolio preparation process is gathering assignments and projects into the *work folder.* The work folder is a file that holds students' work temporarily, until they select items for their portfolio. Students choose work for the work folder at the end of each week by quickly culling items from the week's accumulated papers. We recommend that students keep no more than five to ten items in the work folder at a time. Students are much more discriminating about what has potential than we acknowledge. If a student has left out a piece of work we think represents a developmental milestone, we ask the student if we might keep it in our file for the time being. These papers remain in the work folder until the formal portfolio selection. All other work is sent home.

Parents are accustomed to seeing their child's work come home, and we need to send it home or we will be submerged under accumulating paper. But we should also alert parents to the portfolio process so they understand that we really are assessing children's work. We communicate this to parents in two ways: we send a letter home explaining the process, and we explain it again at Back-to-School Night. The following letter is an example of one we've used.

Dear Parents:

We are very excited to tell you about what's new in our classroom. We will be keeping portfolios that contain pieces that best show your child's learning over a period of time. We will still be sending work papers home, but we will keep selected pieces for the portfolio.

After a period of about six weeks, we will look through all the pieces together, and the student will decide which best represent his or her efforts as a learner over this period. Then we will send this "portfolio" home so that your child can discuss it with you and get your reactions. At the end of the year, your child will have a wonderful record of growth and achievement that we can pass to the next teacher. There will be all kinds of information—journal entries, reading tapes, reactions to readings, creative writing, informational writings from science, social studies, math, art, music, PE, etc. You will see portfolio pieces in all stages of production: some will be just ideas, some will be rough drafts (mistakes and all), and some will be finished products. Not all will be polished. There will be no marks on the papers; if another student or I make a comment or ask a question, we will attach a separate piece of paper to the writing.

I am using portfolios because I believe that students must take responsibility for their own learning and must therefore have a great measure of control all along the way. Our job—yours and mine—is that of facilitator. For my part, I will do my best to create an environment in the classroom where students are free to take risks in learning, to work cooperatively, to be actively involved in their own learning and the assessment of their learning, to take pride in what they produce, and to learn strategies that will serve them long after they have left my class. For your part, we ask that you show an interest in what your child is doing, write a letter to your child and have a conference about his or her portfolio, and be supportive when he or she makes mistakes along the way. We'll give you more specifics when we send the portfolio home for the first time. In this process, we will be building on your child's strengths and helping him or her over the rough spots.

If you have any questions about the portfolio process or if you would like to see the work before it arrives in the portfolio, please come to the classroom and your child will be happy to share it with you.

I thank you in advance for your support.

This is only one example of a letter that might go home. Teachers should send letters that reflect their own classroom and personal teaching style.

Summary

We have talked about the final steps before portfolio selection: gathering baseline data, showing students how to make charts of reading and writing strategies, modeling "Criteria Talk" and sharing the criteria during instruction, deciding on the focus of the student portfolio, and the process of choosing pieces for work folders.

Now we move on to portfolio selection.

CHAPTER FOUR

How Do Students Select Pieces for Their Portfolios?

How do we introduce portfolios?

At the end of October, just before parent-teacher conferences, we are ready to compile the first portfolio. The students have gathered a preliminary selection of papers in their work folders. Now they need some models.

The most effective method we have found for introducing students to the idea of portfolios is to ask members of the community or parents who use portfolios for "real world reasons"—artists, photographers, architects, or designers—to bring their portfolio to class. Presenters can explain how the portfolio represents their work within their profession and discuss their rationale for selecting the materials that are included. Some choose only their best work, while others show the evolution of their work over time.

If a professional portfolio is not available, you can develop a portfolio of your own that expresses who you are as a person outside of school. Include objects, pictures, and examples of writing that represent significant moments in your life or your hobbies and special interests. Be sure to include something that shows your involvement in the learning process, such as an early attempt in painting or sculpture or poetry. Beth, for example, might show her diving log or some photos of her when she was learning to be a scuba diver. Joan might share her private pilot's log and the picture of her standing next to the plane after she soloed for the first time. Attach a short reflection to each item in the portfolio to explain why it tells part of your story and why it is significant. Once they see yours, students will often make this type of portfolio on their own and want to share it with the class.

◼▭ What steps do we take?

Step 1: Portfolio charting

The first step in the portfolio process allows students to step away from their individual work and reflect with the class as a whole on the traits and attributes of good readers and writers. This step involves another charting activity we call *portfolio charting.*

Portfolio charting differs from the instructional charting we discussed in Chapter 2: Portfolio charting allows you step back from the "trees" of individual lessons to look at the "forest" of "accumulated learnings." The teacher writes *What Makes an Expert Writer* and *What Makes a Proficient Reader* one on each of two large pieces of chart paper and then solicits ideas from the students. It is important to record students' ideas in their own words. Using "teacher language" on these charts seems to interfere with the students' sense of ownership of the characteristics you are listing. This charting approach derives from *Portfolio Assessment in the Reading-Writing Classroom* (Tierney, Carter, and Desai 1991, pp. 77–78), but we have expanded on the method described there.

We have collected several examples of portfolio charts from students at different grade levels:

What Makes a Good Reader? (Grade 1)

Going to school
The teacher tells you what it says before you read it
Practice every day
Have someone read to you
Read in school, in the home, and library
You have to be a good thinker

What Do Good Writers Do? (Grade 1)

They put down all the sounds they hear
They put spaces in between words
They write a lot

They practice
They think in their head
Some get tutors
They take their time
Writers don't rush
Good thinkers are good listeners
They work hard and carefully
Good readers make good writers
They try hard
They know a lot of stories
Good readers write a lot
They don't write too much
They try to be good at it
They think before they write

What Good Readers Do (Grade 4)

Sticks with the book
Keeps an eye on the book
Doesn't let distractions get in the way of reading
Sounds out long words
Can tell about a story
Reads many books
Looks up meaning of unknown words
Understands what one reads

What Makes a Good Writer? (Grade 4, taught by Pann Baltz, Disney Teacher of the Year)

Somebody that tells about himself in their writing
Somebody who uses their imagination
Somebody who puts a lot of sense in their writing
Uses facts and good words
Someone who uses the right amount of details
Someone who lets you know that they have lots of things to tell
Someone who puts themself in the character
Someone who writes very specific details
Someone who draws good pictures in the book
Someone who writes exciting words so someone wants to read it
Someone who works really hard on publishing the book
Someone who makes you guess what's going to happen next
Someone who makes you feel like you're really in the story . . . like reality
Someone who puts time into writing the book—not sloppy
Someone who doesn't waste time. They know what they want to achieve

Someone who d   pointing endings
If it's a scary bo   feel really scared
Someone who m   you want to read more and more books
Someone who d   e else's work
Someone who pu   the book
They put a lot of
They put a lot of
They could write
Makes the story in   ing
Someone who teac   ng while they're writing it
Some books have m
There's a meaning t

What Makes a Good Mathematician? (Grade 5)

Wants to learn
Good listening
Doesn't give up
Spends a lot of time studying
Knows times table
Knows how to do decimals
Knows place value
Knows how to line up numbers
Concentrates
Knows problem-solving

What Makes a Good Historian? (Middle School)

A good memory
Likes to study
Goes to places
Has talent
Likes the subject
Is aware of what's going on
Wants to learn about nation's history
Takes notes and studies
Understands people and customs
Wants to read and learn
Asks questions
Attentive

We have included these charts as examples; each classroom chart will look different because it reflects what has happened in instruction up to that time. This is a second valuable service of portfolio charting: the information the students give you mirrors your own instructional clarity. Teachers who talk about processes and strategies in language arts instruction, for example, will get feedback from their students different from that of those whose instruction focuses on correct letter form, exact spelling, or punctuation skills.

Teachers have told us that at first they were reluctant to attempt portfolio charting because they realized that they had not named the processes and strategies as often as they should have during instruction. But when these teachers took a chance and tried their first portfolio chart, they were thrilled by the children's high-level responses. They had underestimated what their students had learned, and many felt renewed confidence in their teaching. At the same time, charting helped them see where they might clarify or supplement their instruction in the future. These charts, which name what proficient readers, expert writers, and learners in the content areas do, provide the criteria the students will use to make selections for their portfolios and write their self-assessments. In Chapter 2 we discussed instructional charting. Portfolio charting represents classroom instruction over a grading period. The semester might begin with a chart on "What expert writers do." Then, as the semester progresses, students will be ready to add specific portfolio charts based on your most recent unit of instruction: "What good poets do" or "What good report writers do."

These charts are posted in the classroom for several weeks. Students know they control the contents and thus are free to revise or add new ideas. When Joan used portfolio charting with her middle school students, they started out with the statement that "writing should be neat." As the semester progressed and they gained experience in writing several drafts, editing, and making corrections and additions, they took the marking pencil and changed the chart to read "writing is messy."

The following three charts are the work of sixth graders, who completed study units on advertising and journalism and then created individual *Time* magazines as the final project:

What Makes a Good Writer?

A good writer:
Needs to have a good imagination
Needs to read to get a good imagination and to pick up a good vocabulary
Interests the reader by using descriptive words and specific nouns
Needs to know how to create a hook for an introduction
The ability to observe (like Robert Frost)

What Good Journalistic Writers Do:

Take notes
Writing based on facts
Why, where, when, what, who, how much, how often, to what extent
Edits details

What Good Advertising Writers Do:

Meaningful words
Eye catching
Use slogans
Good pictures that match slogans
Good imagination
Tell bad things about other products
Creative words/her own words
Creative products/unusual product names

Julie Young, a sixth-grade teacher in Arcadia, California, prepared her students for the *Time* magazine project by introducing the various types of writing that are found in the magazine. She provided instruction and practice in each type of writing. The students followed these criteria in selecting pieces for their portfolios and drew on the language in the charts in writing their self-assessments. At open house, the parents compared the pieces in the magazines with the charts on the wall. The letters that parents wrote to their children showed that this was a highly successful project.

Step 2: Modeling the selection process

Keep in mind that self-assessment is a new experience for most students. Ask an average student (one with a strong ego) if you may use some samples from his or her work folder to model the process for the class. You may be tempted to use writing taken from other sources rather than from your own classroom. We don't recommend this because other writing will not reflect your instruction. Make transparencies of some of the work in the folder. With the class, look at a piece of writing on the overhead projector and help students to name the characteristics of an expert writer they can identify in this example. (Students are not allowed to point out problems in the writing. They may comment only on the "good writer" traits from the portfolio chart.) Point out connections with the traits/criteria on the portfolio charts, write them on a Post-it note, and attach the note to the paper. Students do not at first perceive themselves as writers. Your goal is to guide students to the realization that they demonstrate the traits of proficient readers and writers. We urge you to be realistic in your "teacher" expectations during student self-assessment. Julie Young, in our earlier example, found that she had to be quite specific in directing students' attention to the portfolio chart:

MS. YOUNG: I can see that your writing meets many of the criteria all journalists follow in their reporting. Let's read through the list on the chart and see which ones you've used in your article.

(Student studies the chart.)

MS. YOUNG: Do you know what they are?

STUDENT: I covered the *who, what, where, when,* and *how.* I also wrote facts.

MS. YOUNG: Yes, you did. That's what journalistic writers do. You're becoming a journalistic writer. You may want to choose this piece for your portfolio. Let's write that characteristic on your self-assessment Post-it.

STUDENT: OK.

MS. YOUNG: *(Writes on the Post-it and attaches it to the student's writing.)*

Julie continued to model the process using other pieces of writing from this same student's work folder. When she sensed that the class connected with the process, she asked them get out their own work folders, look over their papers, and try to name one or two of the portfolio criteria in a piece of their own writing. As they did, she circulated throughout the room, helping students individually to make the connection between their writing and the chart.

Ms. Young's students were better able to articulate their ideas on their self-assessments because they had generated specific criteria for the chart. We were disappointed with student self-assessment statements at first because they reverted to traditional criteria, such as "neat work," "good spelling," and "nice illustrations." But as we became more adept at describing the precise criteria for each type of writing during our instruction and conferences, students also became more articulate. Students' self-assessment insights evolve over time. We had to learn to be patient.

Figure 4.1 a–c shows examples of some first-time self-assessment reflections.

Step 3: Making selections and writing self-assessment reflections

Self-assessment is at the very heart of the portfolio! Steps 2 and 3 should be completed on the same day. Once students have had a dry run to practice evaluating their work samples according to the criteria on the portfolio charts (Step 2), they are ready to read over all the selections in their work folders and to decide which items they want to put in their portfolio.

The self-assessment has three possible components (adapted from Tierney, Carter, and Desai 1991, p. 83):

- I chose this because . . .
- I learned . . .
- My goals are . . .

And for grades 1 and 2,

- Next, I want to learn . . .

We have found it more effective to have students write out their own comments rather than limit their responses to a preprinted form. We also recommend large Post-it notes, but any paper is appropriate as long as it stays attached. (Old-fashioned staples and tape work well, too.)

Figure 4.1

Examples of First-Time Self-Assessment Reflections on Post-its

My Story Notebook

Pigs are peiuak.
And They eit.

Thea have periritds funny pechers

Figure 4.1 Continued

My Story Notebook

P. 9

good illustrations
nice handwriting
long storys

I have a dove it lives outside, but it never goes
away. it likes my garden.
It is a white dove.

Once he put one leg up and one leg down.
and I thoght that he lost one leg.
I have 2 fish and they can chag to
brit to dork and they aret eyzy to diy.
They eat alot.

Figure 4.1 Continued

> Very sentence beginnings / Tells about yourself / Uses lots of descriptive words.

I **Dream**

My dream for this country is:
For there to be a lower rate of
crime. Stronger gun control, and you
can't purcase a gun without a licisne.
You also have to belong to a gun club
that teaches you how to use a gun.
That will make fewer drive by
shootings. I want to have fewer
people killed.

In the first round of self-assessment it is easier for students in first through third grades if they confine their comments to "I chose this because . . ." since they might have difficulty naming what they've learned or understanding what we mean by goals. Students in grades four through eight can respond to the first two components, "I chose this because . . ." and "I learned . . ." Goal setting should wait until you have had the opportunity to teach students about goals. We sometimes explain that a goal is something we'd like to do but can't do now. We will discuss this in more detail later.

What are some examples of first self-assessments?

The self-assessment examples were written by students at different grade levels. What about nonreaders and nonwriters? Teachers have approached this problem in three ways:

1. Nonreaders and nonwriters are paired with readers and writers.
2. Children dictate their ideas to the teacher, an aide, or a parent aide.
3. Students from the upper grades come in to take dictation.

(It is important that those who are taking dictation write down students' words verbatim.)

Diana, a first grader, chose two writing samples. On the first (Figure 4.2), she addresses herself: "You put lots of letters." On the second (Figure 4.3), she adds comments on her spelling. Bryant, a second grader, chose one of the stories he wrote on the computer (see previous page).

Alexsander

Today was a horrible day beacase I work up with gum in my hair. I wanted blue and red sneakers with stripes but they wre all solled out so I had to buy plain old, white, sneakers-Icky I sang too loud and had to sit down on my desk. I was scrunch in the middle of the car and I was car sick I threw up all over Tony and I couldn't eat lunch. The dentist said I had cavities and there would have no more candy. Today was a terrible horrible no good very bad day.

"I like this because it was very funny. It is colorful and interesting. Very good illustrations. A lot of details" were his comments on the story.

Wendy chose her report on the San Gabriel Mission (all fourth-grade students in California study the state's history in social studies):

SAN GABRIEL ARCANGEL

The San Gabriel Arcangel is the third mission in founding, fourth northward from San Diego. It was called "Pride of the Missions" because it led all other missions in agriculture. It remained in almost perfect condition, with vineyards that produced fifty thousand gallons of wine per year. Some of the old vines are still there today. San Gabriel became one of the wealthiest missions. It was named after Gabriel, angel of good news.

San Gabriel was founded by Father Pedro Cambon and Father Angel Somera on September 8, 1771. A flood made the padres move the mission in 1775. The new location was only five miles north of the present one. After the war between Governor Jose Echeandia and his successor Manuel Victoria in 1831, the mission became a hospital for the wounded

Figure 4.2

Diana's Writing Sample

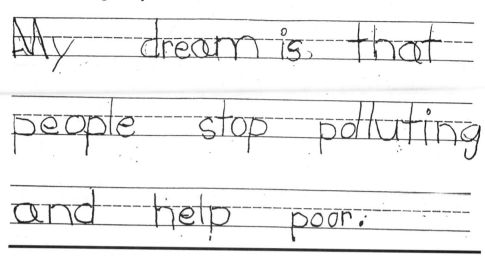

My dream is that people stop polluting and help poor.

Figure 4.3

Diana's Comments on Her Writing Sample

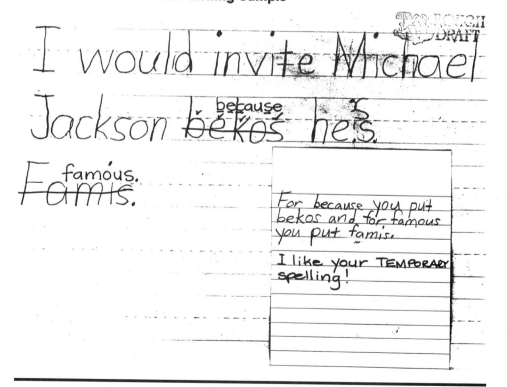

I would invite Michael Jackson ~~bekos~~ because he's ~~Famis~~ famous.

For because you put bekos and for famous you put famis.

I like your TEMPORARY spelling!

men. In the early nineteen hundreds, the mission became the property of the Clareton Fathers. They still own it now and take good care of it.

The architecture of San Gabriel can be traced back to a cathedral in Cordova, Spain. The long, narrow windows are placed high near the roof.

This mission had once been damaged by an earthquake in 1812. It was not repaired until 1828.

This marvelous mission is located on Junipero Street and West Union Drive in the city of San Gabriel.

Wendy commented, "I chose this report because I worked very hard on this, and I'm very proud of it."

What are some reasons students choose particular pieces?

Before students get accustomed to applying the criteria from the portfolio charts in their self-assessment, or in addition to these criteria, they state other, personal reasons for making a particular selection. One of these reasons is the grade they received on the piece. We know that teachers grade student papers, but we recommend that grades not be placed directly on the front. We put our grades and comments on a separate sheet of paper, because students who are new to the portfolio process may be inclined to base their selection on grades. Students accustomed to traditional grades often find it difficult to assess their *own* learning. If assignments must be graded at the intermediate and junior high levels, the grades should be written on the back of the paper. Students who choose a paper because it received a good grade will still need to state the reason for their choice in terms of the criteria their selection has met.

Other personal reasons for particular choices include:

- being able to do something today that they could not do yesterday
- using a strategy for the first time
- changing from one strategy to a more effective strategy
- trying "really hard"
- discovering that a piece is—or has become—personally meaningful
- choosing their best work

What kind of comments do students use for "I learned . . ."

The "I learned . . ." aspect of selection is always more difficult for students. It requires a lot of teacher modeling and student practice. Yet with each portfolio experience it becomes easier, because teachers begin to use "criteria talk" every day and often encourage students to think about what they learned during conferences. A teacher can direct the students to the charts as well as to their own journals and learning logs.

Lindsy, one of Mrs. Ambler's sixth-grade students, wrote this assessment of her writing:

There are a lot of things that I have learned in Writing [Class] this year from September to February. I have learned to make interviews to people, ask them the important questions, then gather the data, reorganize the materials and start writing. I have learned to make observations, in which some are just casual observations, and yet some are very keen observations. I have learned to use my five senses sometimes while I am writing a piece of writing, as in the case of writing "Brownie in Terabithia." I have used my eyes, my nose, my hands, my ears as well as my mouth during the whole writing process. I have learned to use similes and metaphors in my writing, which has been very challenging and interesting and definitely has helped to make the writing alive and more of a real-life event! I have also learned to carefully record the events in sequence, as in the case of writing "The Fastest Kid in Sixth Grade" in which the whole class and Mrs. Ambler have different races, in different categories. Last but not least, I have learned to really enjoy and love writing, which in turn will last me my whole life long.

The authors that have inspired me the most are Katherine Patterson, E. B. White and Charles Dickens. I like the way they use words; the descriptions in the stories; the ways the stories had drawn my [whole] attention; and also, the morals behind the stories.

I have seen my growth in writing. I must use more descriptive words, similes, as well as metaphors. I have tried to make the stories more realistic. I have tried to put my point of view, and I have tried to use more vocabulary, and good grammar so the readers have no problem reading my writing.

Lindsy's teacher is an expert at naming and charting instruction, clarifying the criteria for each assignment during instruction, and using this same language when she writes evaluations. It is not surprising that Lindsy is able to articulate clearly what she has learned.

How do we help students set goals?

Because students need to learn the significance of goal setting, this step can wait until the second portfolio selection. "What I want to learn next . . ." may be as new to students as writing self-assessments, but most students arc aware of what they want to learn next because they have assimilated ideas from listening to the teacher talk with other students. Many of the items students include in their goal statements can be found on the portfolio charts.

Early primary-level students may need a lot of discussion about what it means to set goals for themselves before they can be expected to do it independently. The portfolio conference, when both the teacher and the student record their goals on the conference form, offers an opportunity for individual discussion. Randy, a third-grade student in a special class, recorded his goal:

I woold like to stay in this class and lirn to rite beder and it is verry inpomitit [important].

A fourth grader named Patty noted:

I would like to lern how to read better. I hope I can get better grades in reading langus [language]. I wish I can wriht longer paregraphes and better poems.

Josh, a fifth grader, wrote:

I would like to get better at reading and writting skills. Over the summer time I got rusty at some things.

Miguel, in sixth grade, decided:

I want to get out of this class to learn how to read on a 9th or 10th grade leval. I can read a little 8th grade leval. An I would like to write like an author.

Dennis, a seventh grader, felt confident enough to risk telling the teacher about how hard it is for him to read out loud in class.

I would like to be able to read better. I would like to have the fun and excitement of reading. I would like to read Steven King Books, but I can't because When I read small letters I get headaches. I also stop reading long books because I'm not patient enough. When I read I try to keep the book under 115 pages so I won't get bored with the book. I want be able to read in front of the class without studdering. When I studder I feel like the whole class is laughing at me. I also want to get over my fear of reading. When ever the class is reading outloud in front of the class I keep saying to myself don't pick me, don't pick me.

Tran is a also a seventh grader, but he has a lot more confidence in his ability than Dennis:

I think my reading skills have been a lot better since I first started I think I got better by skimming and skipping a word. In writing I think that I can write a lot more.

Next year I will use the skills you have given me and I will know how to write better and take notes better.

Jerry, an eighth grader, is also the class clown, but his heart was in the right place when he wrote the following for his pre-algebra class:

Personal Goals for the 4th Quarter

1. Neater Notes, Neater Work, Neater Homework
2. Talk Less
3. Listen More

OUTLINE
4th Quarter

1. Neater Work
    a. class notes
    b. class work
    c. homework
2. Talk Less
    a. worry less about what friends are doing
    b. joke around less
3. Listen More
    a. pay more attention to teacher instead of friends
    b. take more classnotes

What are some additional hints for Step 3?

To encourage student success in portfolio selection, we recommend the following:

■ Invite as many adults and teacher aides as possible to the classroom to facilitate student thinking and focus on the criteria. Teachers and aides can move from one student to the next asking leading questions and helping children connect what they have done to items on the expert writer or proficient reader list. We need to make sure, however, that we don't put words into students' mouths: we want to preserve student ownership of the portfolio.

■ When you are evaluating individual assignments, record your own comments, grades, and suggestions on a separate piece of paper or write them on the back of the student's work. In this way, your evaluation will not influence the student's thinking during assessment.

■ Remind students that work does not have to be in its final form in order to be valuable for the portfolio. Work that demonstrates a new strategy or a first attempt at a new process can be included even if it is not perfect. Work can also be valued for its "risk taking" or creativity; sometimes the milestone worth recognizing is the *trying*.

■ To inspire excitement about the process, videotape students as they make their portfolio selections and interview them about their choices. Parents might volunteer for this task. The video verifies the significance of the portfolio, and, as a result, students recognize its importance.

What if students leave out a significant piece of work?

Not all students will select work that shows significant milestones in their learning, and this is to be expected. Students are not professional assessors. In view of this fact, we always keep a folder for each student's work in our file. When we observe a student doing something significant for the first time, or doing it exceptionally well, we put a star on the Post-it. This lets students know that if they do not choose this work for their portfolio, we want it for our file because it is significant. We try to be specific about why it is worth keeping in our file. This honors student ownership and control of choices, but it also ensures that we won't lose track of a sample of significant growth. We can negotiate with the student about whether or not to show the piece to parents.

Are portfolios worth the time?

When we first began developing portfolios, we were concerned about the time required for portfolio charting and self-assessment writing. Like most teachers, we felt pressured to cover the text or the curriculum. But once we began to see students becoming actively involved in their own learning, we realized that these activities provided one of the most significant aspects of the learning cycle. When students feel empowered, they change their attitudes about learning; this happens literally the day after they first write self-assessment reflections. Beth asked Lori, a new fifth-grade teacher, if she had observed any differences after her students made their portfolio selections. It was as exciting to hear her discoveries about the power of self-assessment as it was to see her students begin recognizing themselves as writers:

> Well, let me tell you, I saw a huge difference at several points along the way, and I think it started when we generated the list [portfolio chart]! I was shocked at the things that they said on the list. I was surprised because you never really know how directly you're saying these things to them. But it came out great. Well, that was the first thing, the way the list went together so well. But what surprised me much more was once they had that list, how empowered they became. Now, I had heard that might happen, but I really didn't really buy into it and nobody ever said it would happen to the degree that it did. The kids immediately took control of their writing. Immediately! They were talking and telling me what they were needing to do, what they were supposed to do, what they were trying to do. Which is so shocking because since they came up with this list, I know they knew those things, yet they didn't belong to them until they made that list. I think that that was the distinction and that changed ownership. They came up with their own standards and it really changed the way they approached their writing. It was amazing! I couldn't wait to tell you this because it really blew me away!

The portfolio chart that Lori's students produced reflects the qualities of her teaching:

What Do Good Writer's Do? (Grade 5)

Prewriting:
Brainstorm
Take time to think
Choose specific topic
Write about things they are familiar with
Feel optimistic and confident about writing

Writing:
Stick to the subject
Make detail sentences relate to topic sentences
Explain things thoroughly
Express their feelings in writing
Make their stories seem real
Give examples
Use descriptive words & phrases
Use a variety of words (not just simple & plain words)
Include proper punctuation

After writing first draft:
Proofread: (punctuation, spelling, proper paragraphs, sentence form)
Enjoy sharing their stories
Feel proud of their work

▄▄▭ Summary

We have talked about the need to provide models for portfolios and reviewed the steps in the portfolio process: charting the criteria, modeling the selection process, selecting pieces and writing reflections, and finally, setting goals.

Now we look at sharing portfolios with peers, teachers, and parents.

CHAPTER FIVE

What Is Involved in Conferences?

How do we prepare for the portfolio conference?

When students have selected items for their portfolios, the next step in the portfolio process is preparing for a portfolio conference, first with a peer, then with the teacher and parents. During the preparation students organize their selections in order of priority and decide which aspects of the portfolio they want to discuss during the conference. Once they have decided on the order, they write a letter of introduction to any potential readers of their portfolio.

What might some introductory letters look like?

The introductory letter should introduce the reader to the creator of the portfolio and describe its significance. At this point, students may also want to design a cover or a special folder or box in which to keep their work. (We'll talk more about storage later on in the chapter.) Students in grades five and up can do this preparation at home. Here are some sample letters:

Introduction

Doing the I-Search Project [investigating family history] has made me realize how lucky I am to have such a wonderful family. I have been interviewing all of my family members. It has been very interesting to me.

All of my family suffered through World War II. All of my family members are immigrants from Russia. They left for many reasons such as communism, lack of food, anti-Semitism, and many more reasons. My maternal great-grandmother and my paternal grandparents were the most interesting part of researching my project. The paternal and maternal sides of my family both have interesting backgrounds. My parents told me some very interesting stories like my family in the Zionist movement, wars, and concentration camps. I enjoyed hearing these stories.

In my portfolio I included poems about my family, family crests, a Mr. Thurstone report, interviews from members of my family, and poems about myself. From these, I have found out information about my family heritage. I traced as far back as my great-great-great-grandparents. I enjoyed learning this.

I have enjoyed doing my I-Search Project on my family heritage. It has been very fun and educational for me. I hope that the reader enjoys it just as much as I do.

Michelle, 6th grader

Introduction Letter

To whom it may concern,

This is a letter to explain what I'm putting in my Math Portfolio. The first thing, this letter, is to explain clearly, what is in my portfolio. Second, are the portfolio questions which will let you know how well I'm doing in math and what I think about it. Third, the three homework assignments let you know how well I know these three concepts and how well I can calculate them. Next, the difficult concept, shows you a concept I had trouble with and how I've improved by calculating a problem correctly. Next, the self evaluation, tells you how well I think I'm doing in math. Last, the parent feedback tells you how well my parents think I'm doing in math.

Tran, 7th grader

Introduction

What I'm about to share to you is not just any portfolio. It's more then a bunch of papers in a folder. It represents charisma, effort, and dedication. It includes poems, stories, and pictures. What you will find in this portfolio are summaries, poems about our own magical place, stories on incidents, and special tasks which you will see inside. I guess you're wondering what this project is all about. Well, we read a book called Bridge to Terabithia. Mrs. Ambler, our teacher, gave us many assignments on it. I hope you enjoy every poem and story you read.

Eric, 6th grader

Pre-Algebra

This is my completed portfolio self-evaluation. I feel that I have completed my portfolio with all the items requested and have done them to the best of my ability. I have learned much this quarter and my portfolio sums it all up. I have enjoyed putting this portfolio together and if it were up to me to give myself a grade I would make it an A. My portfolio shows my best work.

Maria, 8th grader

Introduction

Eighth grade at school has not only been a year of science, math, history and French, but also a year of English: the Arts. The pilot program has included many interesting activities which enhances everyone's writing abilities.

This year, I feel, I have written much more than in the past. A few assignments have brought out my strong points, and strengthened my weak ones. One assignment brought out my ability to write unique similes and metaphors: the *Ultimatum.* Some other ones created new images in my mind.

My favorite writing genre is the poem. Most of my works in this portfolio are poems. Try to create your own images or interpret mine. . .and have fun!

Brett, 8th grader

Dear reader,

You are about to embark on a journey through my progression on what I have learned in this class. As you travel you will find new strategies I have learned and how I successfully applied them to some of my other classes, new knowledge I have mastered, and examples of improvement and effort that have paid off. In each one you will find a self-assessment that explains why I chose it, what I learned from it, and what my goal is in that area. After seeing it all you should get a pretty good picture of what I have accomplished in becoming a master student.

Gary, 8th grader

What is involved in peer conferences?

Peer conferences are a time for students to rehearse their self-assessment ideas in preparation for the conferences with teachers and parents or simply to get feedback on their portfolio. First, we prepare students by establishing the purpose and the parameters of the peer conference. Since children at all ability levels will be sharing their work with one another, the most important guideline is that all remarks or observations must focus on what has been accomplished, not on weaknesses or errors. During the discussion of guidelines for peer conferences, it is a good idea to differentiate between a *peer editing conference* and a *peer portfolio conference.* While the peer editing conference focuses on an individual piece of writing and includes suggestions for improvement, the peer portfolio conference focuses on the portfolio's record of learning over time.

Second, together with the class, we lay down conference ground rules to keep the bruised egos and the bloodshed to a minimum:

Let your partner hold his or her own portfolio.
Give positive feedback first and suggestions for improvement afterward.
Ask questions instead of judging.
Respect the other person's efforts.

To model a practice peer conference, we usually ask for a volunteer. Then, using the ground rules, we role-play a discussion of one student's portfolio. The other students observe and then discuss their observations. At this point the teacher models the kinds of questions that will allow the owner of the portfolio to talk about the significance of his or her learning:

Why did you choose your first piece?
What other kinds of pieces have you selected for your portfolio?
What piece do you plan to share with the teacher?
What do you think you learned?
Did you discover that you learned any new strategies?

Next, the teacher gives students some tips on how to fill out the Peer Portfolio Conference Form (see A.5 in Appendix A) and asks for two more volunteers who have already looked at each other's portfolio and can discuss them knowledgeably. The students use the same format the teacher used and share the Peer Portfolio Conference Form. Figures 5.1 and 5.2 offer examples.

Depending on the comfort level of the students and their sensitivity, you may have to do further modeling of these conferences. Good peer conference interactions develop over time. In our experience, it is better for the teacher to choose the pairings for the first round to be sure a troubled learner does not like up with an insensitive partner. Later, as students learn what is expected, they can choose their own partners.

Figure 5.1

Andrea's Peer Portfolio Conference Form

Name _Andrea_

Owner of the portfolio _Kim_

Date _March 6, 1997_

I am most impressed by _the cover page._
It's very artistic

My favorite entry in the portfolio is _the acrostic_
poem because _She used new vocabulary words_
Kim shows strengths in the following areas of
reading or writing: _She uses good hooks_
to interest the reader in her story

Recommendations I would make for next time _to_
organize her portfolio more carefully.

Additional Comments:

Designate a corner where students can discuss their reflections with one another but without disturbing students who are still writing their self-assessments. The teacher needs to monitor these first conference attempts so that students can discuss how well they understood what they were supposed to do and how well they followed the guidelines. If the first round does not go well, the teacher needs to stop here and initiate more modeling. (Have patience. Peer conferences are a difficult concept for students to grasp—but worth it.)

In any portfolio conference, the partner's primary purpose is to listen to the portfolio owner discuss his or her own views about his learning. The listener shares in this celebration and points out other positive aspects of growth and progress.

Figure 5.2

Hector's Peer Portfolio Conference Form

Name _Hector_

Owner of the portfolio _Pablo_

Date _May 6, 1997_

I am most impressed by _the creative poems and the wonderful use of words_

My favorite entry in the portfolio is _his letter to the author_ because _he shows how to write persuasively_

Pablo shows strengths in the following areas of reading or writing:

editing, organization, he reads great mysteries

Recommendations I would make for next time _to add more illustrations_

Additional Comments: _a real masterpiece!_

What is involved in teacher preparation for portfolio conferences with students?

We remember feeling overwhelmed when we first started portfolio conferences because discussing individual strengths and areas of growth with thirty or more students seemed too large a task for our memories and our schedules. We had to step back to recognize how much purposeful reading and writing students were actually doing. We felt it was one of the most valuable times of the whole year.

   Talking about self-assessment nails down learning in a way other methods don't.

One secret for developing confidence in one's ability to hold effective conferences and not rely solely on memory is to keep good records throughout the grading period. These records might include

- notes taken during reading and writing conferences
- notes taken during shared book discussions
- your notebook, which contains anecdotal records based on observations you've made
- checklists of developmental milestones
- the baseline information forms from September
- your grade book

These records will provide a clear idea of each child's growing strengths and needs from week to week and from month to month. Clearly, traditional grade books do not lend themselves to writing about each student's work (a *B* grade doesn't tell which criteria were met and which were not), but the grades may tell you something about the student's effort and whether or not he or she is turning in assignments.

Scheduling portfolio conferences is important. The teacher needs time to prepare for each conference by studying the portfolio selections and self-assessments, and reflecting on the student's growth and progress.

In order to increase our efficiency, we jot a few notes, shown in Figure 5.3 on the Portfolio Conference Form in preparation for each conference (see A.6 in Appendix A for blank version).

How do we conduct the conferences?

Once we've prepared, we're ready for the actual conferences. We try to meet students in a corner of the classroom where there's not too much activity. We honor the student's ownership by having the student hold his or her own portfolio. The student can also have ownership of the conference if the teacher allows the conversation to revolve around the student's portfolio choices and self-assessment reflections. Ownership is not easy for students to understand because they have relied on the teacher to talk and to judge their work. During the first part of the conference the teacher listens while the student articulates his or her thoughts. Because self-reflections are the student's perceptions of how his or her learning has met the criteria for proficient readers and writers, self-assessment reflections should be not judged as right or wrong.

Students don't always know how to begin. Here are some starter questions:

- What would you like to share?
- What kinds of pieces have you selected for your portfolio?
- What will a reader learn about you from your portfolio?
- What new learning does your portfolio show?

Figure 5.3

Portfolio Conference Notes

Name _____Chris_____

Subject/type of entry _____6th grade language arts_____

Date _____May_____

Key:	+ = excellent
	✓+ = very good
	✓ = good
	✓- = fair
	- = poor

Student's reflections on:
- ability to write book responses

Criteria that were met:
- book responses of more than 2 sentences

Areas of growth:
- has several possible choices of book responses for portfolio

Areas for development:
- needs to use more descriptive language

Teacher's reflections:
- doesn't care for writing narrative text; likes content material, but is very aware of his need to be able to write in different genres; beginning to take some risks writing narratives; needs better book choices to get him hooked

Areas of growth:
- ___✓-___ eagerness to share portfolio
- ___✓___ organization of portfolio
- ___✓___ connecting to the criteria
- ___✓+___ insight into learning

Student's goals:
- have spelling more under control so that writing is easier; read better books

Teacher's goals for the student:
- take more risks with spelling using the computer; choose more interesting books; be more accepting of his own work—look at growth rather than weaknesses

- How does the writing in this portfolio compare to your first writing sample?
- How has your writing changed?
- What can you do now that you couldn't do before?

Some additional facilitating questions might include

- What area is strongest [name of genre in reading or writing that was the most current focus of instruction, e.g., poetry, biography, science fiction]?
- How do the choices in your portfolio show your new strategies?
- What things did you learn about yourself in developing this portfolio?
- Which aspects of your reading and writing improved?
- Which criteria of proficient readers and writers of [strategy or genre] are seen in your work?
- Which criteria did you satisfy that caused you to select this piece of work?
- What does it show about you as a learner (in science, math, social studies, art, PE, as well as language arts)?
- What was your purpose in choosing this topic, project?
- Did you accomplish your purpose?
- What would you do differently?
- What special knowledge or interest did you use to make this project meaningful?
- What obstacles did you overcome to make it meaningful?
- If this is a "best work" piece, explain the process you followed to make it a best work.
- Now that you have evaluated this piece of work, what criteria would you strive to meet next time you do this type of assignment or project?
- What are your goals for reading? for writing? for subject areas?

Many students will underestimate their strengths and find it difficult to name criteria they have fulfilled. They may not recognize that they have begun to write or read using a new strategy. This is an opportunity for the teacher to say, "I've noticed other new developments, processes, strategies, that you are developing. Did you know that you are beginning to . . . and . . .? Look at the portfolio charts. You are beginning to develop the first three criteria on the proficient reader's chart!"

Some students will talk freely. We have found that this willingness is directly related to the "risk" quotient encouraged in the classroom. If the teacher honestly names and discusses his own learning, it also encourages students to be open. We might say, "I see that you're having some difficulty writing an introduction to this piece. When I was in fifth grade, I had the same problem."

What do we do with students who present special problems?

Some teachers are uncomfortable with students who say little or are unable to articulate their thoughts quickly. It is an art for teachers to remain quiet, wait with confidence, and give the student think time. We often find that when we wait, we receive information that is surprisingly rich in insight.

A common question teachers ask is "What do I say to that student who doesn't do his or her work and rarely hands in an assignment?" Some students do seem unable to learn new strategies. Others are completely unmotivated. Invariably, though, if we direct the student to specific evidence of change by comparing current work to work from the preceding September, the student will be able to recognize something positive. While the student may not be working up to the standards for that class or grade level, some progress in writing is not unusual. Be sure to point out each item that shows growth and avoid comparisons with others.

We have been told by many of these struggling students that the portfolio conferences were some of the most meaningful feedback times they had ever had with a teacher.

Students confirm our observation that most other assessment opportunities produce only negative feedback for some of them.

Scott is a case in point. He was as unmotivated as they come, a tough kid in any class. A frustrated nonreader and nonwriter, even at the fifth-grade level, he had such problems with word attack skills, it appeared doubtful that he would ever be able to read or spell successfully. He also had problems expressing himself verbally. In fact, most of the time he was cantankerous. With lots of patient encouragement, however, he gradually began to take responsibility for his own learning. The following portfolio conference reflects his growth in writing over several years. Given his difficulties, the portfolio became a graphic example—to him and to us—of what he was able to accomplish. The portfolio was a good reminder: we should never underestimate its power to motivate kids! When the teacher asked Scott how he feels now, he said "happy." (That was an understatement: he was floating!) Scott's work samples are followed by the text of his conference.

Sample 1 (Dictated)

There was a man in the snow in the Yukon. It was snowing for a while. There was ice under the snow. He was walking through the snow with a dog. He was starting to freeze. He had his food under his shirt by his skin so it wouldn't get cold. He had a beard and it was keeping him safe from the snow a little bit. He kept walking. He was thinking about his friends and about if there was a fire because he was starting to freeze on his hands and his arms. He kept trying to light the fire. He was starting to get hungry so he ate his buns. Then after that he started walking again, then his legs started to freeze and he couldn't move. He tried to light the fire, but he couldn't. He froze so much that he died. The dog ran off to the camp.

Sample 2 (A journal entry)

I WENT TO THE MALL. I WEMT OUT WITH A GIRL.

Sample 3 (A journal entry)

I went to my gllse houme and I went to the FS and I wnet to my frse houme there I went houme.

Sample 4 (A story written on a computer with a spell-checker)

I got my classes and at lunchtime I left campus. I got Metals, math, reading, P.E. I didn't dress P.E. because I didn't want to. They said fine, do what you want to do.

Sample 5 (A journal entry)

I wate skating, and I bought a naw skat. I waht to my Gait house. I waht skating in San Francisco, and I skating there, and I play on my computer. I waht to my girls haouse. I want to swim, and I waht to get food. and I took it to the football gane.

Sample 6 (A journal entry on the computer)

My favorite sport is football. And my favority ronnle loh. I fights and yelling. Then tackie. And the other guis like Roger Craig Ricky Ellison Gvarterback—Todd Marinovich suck. be they are from the former 49ers. Annd the las Football Superbowl—Won in 1983. One touchdown in a score is 6 points. And one point after is 1 point.

Sample 7 (A report, shortened)

When and why was the Civil War fought?
   The war began in 1860 and it ended in 1865. The president was Abraham Lincoln. Lincoln chose to keep all states in the United States, and he was against slavery. He fought the war to end all mischief. He said that a country divided would fall.
   The South fought because they didn't like the government telling them what to do. Second, they wanted to keep slaves and they wanted to get out of the Union. They wanted slaves to do their dirty work: cotton picking and clean their houses.

Which states fought for the South?
   Texas, Virginia, North Carolina, South Carolina, Louisiana, Arkansas, Mississippi, Alabama, Florida, Tennessee, and Georgia.

Who were the generals?
   Robert E. Lee was the Confederate general who commanded all the Southern troops. Ulysses S. Grant was the general who was the commmander of all the Union troops for the North.

(Scott has various samples of writing laid out in front of him in sequential order.)

TEACHER: What do you notice about this piece of writing compared to your early writing?

SCOTT: At the beginning of the year, I was dictating because I didn't like writing.

TEACHER: I remember how you felt about writing then; you really hated it! Do you remember why you hated it so much?

SCOTT: I was scared when I started to write on my own because it was scary.

TEACHER: Why was it scary?

SCOTT: I thought I'd make mistakes and wouldn't do it so well.

TEACHER: Now that you're looking at your work, how do you feel about it? Are you proud?

SCOTT: Yeah! *(Gets a big satisfied grin on his face.)*

TEACHER: Let's look at some later pieces of writing and see what you've learned.

SCOTT: *(Reads quietly)* I'm still a 49er fan. *(Commenting on the topic)* It's full of bigger words. I can see a difference between the first pieces and the last. I can tell I liked football a lot.

TEACHER: What happened when you wrote about topics you knew about?

SCOTT: It becomes clear.

TEACHER: And I can see you obviously knew a lot about football because you wrote a lot on that topic.

SCOTT: *(He reads some more of his selections.)* I always write about seeing my friends, and my writing is clearer.

TEACHER: You mean the penmanship?

SCOTT: Yeah. *(He points to an early writing sample and compares it to a later one.)*

TEACHER: *(He picks up another piece of writing that is a journal entry.)* Oh, I think this was better.

TEACHER: I see something that good writers do. Do you know what it is?

SCOTT: No.

TEACHER: I see sequence. You put the events of the day in order. Next, why don't you check the spelling. Do you see any differences?

SCOTT: Oh, yeah. It's better. And I got periods and commas. I musta been all excited about middle school when I wrote this. I think this was a story. I hated to write stories. I was by myself. I didn't have spell check. I musta been happy that day.

TEACHER: I see that you picked your report on the Civil War for your last piece of writing. What do you think about that compared to your earlier pieces?

SCOTT: *(Looking at it)* It took forever because I really worked on it. I learned a lot. This was fun because I'm interested in history. I just wanted to get the other writing over with.

TEACHER: What would you like to be able to do now? What is your goal?

SCOTT: My spelling needs improvement.

TEACHER: Maybe we can work on both editing and proofreading strategies. Those would include working on finding misspelled words and correcting them. Your confidence in writing has grown, but maybe we need to continue to work on that.

We serve students like Scott best when we allow them to keep portfolios over a longer period of time than just one year. Their growth is usually slow but steady. They need to be reminded about where they started to see how far they've progressed.

What about second language learners?

Students with special needs also include our second language learners. Research in the area of English-as-a-Second Language shows that portfolios help with intercultural communication (Hashem 1995), help to build partnerships with students around goals (Smolen et al. 1995), provide assistance for language production and fluency (Caldwell and Downs 1995), and nurture student learning (Gottlieb 1995).

Portfolios are an effective way to measure students' growth in language learning. This is particularly true for portfolios that include audiotapes of both speaking and reading. Having a record of their spoken as well as their written language gives students a graphic picture of where they've been and how much they've grown. It's especially helpful to tape-record the actual portfolio conferences. These tapes can provide a running assessment from conference to conference. Listening to the tape of the previous conference and comparing the student's current speech and language can form the basis for the conference. Another positive feature of this method is that these tapes can be sent home to parents.

What about goal setting?

The last part of the conference should be spent on goal setting, first by the student and then by the teacher. Fill in the Portfolio Conference Notes form (see A.6 in Appendix A) together and record the areas the student wants to set as goals for the next term. With goal setting, students can no longer be passive observers. They have to become active participants in the learning process.

Setting goals further enhances student ownership of learning.

Students need to be encouraged to be specific when setting goals. "Becoming a better writer" is very general; "I want to learn how to write introductory paragraphs" is more specific. Goals should be attainable and should relate to the student's next level of development in reading and writing. The following are examples of meaningful goals new portfolio developers set for themselves:

Kindergarten	I want to color in the lines.
Grade 1	I want to make better spaces between words.
Grade 2	I want to read a whole book.
Grade 3	I want to write a story with a beginning, middle, and end.
Grade 4	I want to write note cards for writing reports without copying from the encyclopedia.
Grade 5	I want to remember what I read.
Grade 6	I want to talk with my friends in class less and stop getting in trouble with the teacher.
Grade 7	I want to use more metaphors in my poetry.
Grade 8	I would like to increase my reading speed.

Because goals are noted on the Conference Form, they remain part of the record. At each conference, students can evaluate whether they have met the goals they set during the previous conference. In addition, you may see some common problems that extend beyond one particular student and might decide to plan some whole class instruction around these areas, for example, maintaining the same verb tense throughout a paper or putting capitals at the beginning of sentences. (For further references on the topic of student goals, see Hansen (1992).

■■▭ How do we manage conferences?

Students can sign up for portfolio conferences when they are prepared (in the primary grades the teacher may want to assign times). Allow ten to fifteen minutes for each conference. In our experience, when the teacher is conducting portfolio conferences, options for activities students can do if they finish their work early must be stated very clearly. It's most effective if the teacher and the students compile this list of options together. Such a list might include some of the following:

What to Do During Conference Time

Make your own decisions.
Ask a neighbor for help.
Go to a learning center.
Do research on the computer.
Read a book.

Work on a piece of writing.

Write in journals.

Draw a picture to go with my reading or writing.

Work on the next step of a project.

Do my homework.

As we stated in our discussion of baseline conferences in Chapter 3, the bottom line for effective conference management is helping students realize that conferences are sacred. They may not be interrupted by anyone (save for an emergency call to 911). Kids soon get the message: the teacher will not answer their questions, but will direct them to the chart to make their own decisions.

Teachers who have a hundred or more students may find it difficult to meet with every student during every grading period. But there are alternatives. The first is to schedule short conferences in which the teacher moves her chair from one student's desk to the next (Joan calls this the "have chair, will travel" conference). Conference time can be limited to five minutes and to only one aspect of a student's portfolio. Even in this short time a teacher will be able to address the student's strengths and future goals. A second alternative is to confer with one half of the students and write the other half a letter in response to their written reflections. The letter can be brief but personal, and contain information you would tell the student directly if he or she were sitting next to you.

The importance of writing a letter or having a conference with every student is best illustrated by this story. An excellent language arts teacher told us about John, one of the best writers in her eighth grade class, who came to her to ask her for her opinion of his writing ability. She was surprised at the question, because she felt that she *had* been telling him for several months, every time she handed back his work, how much she rejoiced in his exceptional writing ability! The conversation sounded like this:

TEACHER: Why, John, don't you know that I'm always excited to read your work because you have so much natural talent?

JOHN: Oh no *(looking surprised)*. I had no idea that you thought that. You've never told me that.

The teacher remarked that if a talented student like John didn't know how she felt about his ability, imagine what little positive input the struggling writers must have thought they were getting from her! She felt she had really failed as a teacher on that score!

After that, she wrote a personal letter to every student if she could not manage to schedule conference time.

Her students treasured those letters, and they often became permanent additions to their portfolios.

Should you doubt the importance of writing a letter to each student, try this:

Write down the name of a teacher in your own experience as a student in grades 1 to 12 who told you about your strengths as a learner or just as a human being. Then write down the name of a teacher during those same years who listened to your self-evaluation, valued your opinions about your learning, and asked you to set your own goals. We have polled hundreds of teachers informally and received approximately one or two positive responses per hundred. When these few teachers tell their stories, naming the strengths their teachers discussed with them, their memories are as vivid as yesterday because the experience was so rare and so meaningful. Most also said that they have become strong and confident in that very learning area.

Before we leave the subject of middle school students, we would like to mention a current popular trend: student-led conferences for older students. Since student-led conferences require extensive preparation, we felt they were beyond the scope of this book. For helpful resources, see the work of Terri Austin (1994) and Carol Santa (1995).

How can we schedule time for portfolio selection and portfolio conferences?

The most common question about portfolios is how to find time. A first step is to recognize the value of portfolios. Teachers who have observed the empowering effects of portfolios have told us that the portfolio process actually increased the quality of their students' learning connections. They didn't hesitate to drop other activities.

Value for value, the portfolio ensures a new level of quality in learning.

Beth remembers one first-grade teacher who claimed that she couldn't possibly fit portfolio selection time into her scheduling. "After all," she said looking out at her students, who were totally involved, "all they are doing is reading and writing." Beth could see her eyes say, "Oops!"

For students of any age reading, evaluating, and writing portfolio assessments can replace the planned language arts lesson on one or two days in a grading period. Learning to write a meaningful assessment, and supporting it, is after all, a "real world" type of writing. Making selections requires analytical thinking and encourages discovery of one's own abilities and learning. This is valuable! The following sample schedules offer ideas for making time. Figure 5.4 shows a sample schedule for primary classes, Figure 5.5 a sample schedule for intermediate classes.

Looking at the proposed schedule, you can see that there are reading, writing, and portfolio conferences scheduled throughout the day. Toward the end of the grading period, each of these conference times can be devoted to portfolios. A summary of the complete portfolio process appears in Chapter 6. Sample record

Figure 5.4

Sample Schedule: Primary

Mon	Tues	Wed	Thurs	Fri

USSR (Uninterrupted Silent Sustained Reading)
READING CONFERENCES

Big Books, Shared Book Experience with Book Response
Journals & Writing   Workshop with Direct Instruction
(Informal Conferences/Teachable Moments)
RECESS
Math

| Art | Penmanship/Creative | Drama/PE | Music |

LUNCH
Teacher Read-aloud

Social Studies, Science, or Thematic Unit (Integrated)
Portfolio Selection   Conference
RECESS

Library, Sports, Portfolio Conferences
(Friday) Self-evaluation/Peer/Teacher

---

sheets for peer, parent, and teacher portfolio conferences appear in Appendix A (A.8, A.9, A.10).

Managing the time for portfolios is a matter of pacing. Set aside one period every week so that students can sort through the week's assignments in their work folder. Do not have them begin making actual portfolio selections from the work folder or write self-assessments until the fourth and fifth week. This allows them plenty of time to accumulate several pieces of writing and reading in the current genre or study unit as well as ample practice time to develop new reading and writing strategies.

How do early primary teachers manage this process?

Even if your students are not reading and writing, it does not mean that you cannot try portfolios. Early primary teachers need to schedule portfolio time when the maximum number of teacher aides and parents are available to help students write their assessments. Many mini-conferences can take place as the adults move from

Figure 5.5

Sample Schedule: Middle School

Mon	Planning and Instructional Time with Students Journals (Informal Conferences/Teachable Moments)
Tues	Instructional Time/Cooperative Learning Groups
Wed	Instructional Time Journals Peer Conferences/Teacher Conferences Integrating Reading/Writing
Thurs	Integrating Reading/Writing Informal Observations/Conferences
Fri	Journals, Work Folder Selections
	Portfolio Conferences—Peer/Teacher Self-evaluation
	Last Week of Semester: Parent Portfolio Conferences Portfolio Party!

one student to the next, guiding them to focus on their work and how it relates to the criteria on the portfolio charts. Some may conclude that a high level of assessment may not be occurring, but Beth found exactly the opposite when she interviewed a class of first graders. They had just finished making their first portfolio selections, and this is what some of them said:

"I got better when I was doing more."
"I learned how to spell more words."
"I discovered that I can write a whole story without squiggly lines" [for words they could not spell].
"I discovered that I could spell good."

When the teacher brought her students to the playground for recess the next day, she discovered two of her recess-loving rascals sitting in their seats writing when she returned to the classroom. She asked them why in world they hadn't gone out for recess, and they told her that it said on that portfolio chart that good writers write more, so they were writing more!

How do we involve the parents in portfolios?

Portfolios take the mystery out of assessment for parents. They support the report card, giving hard-copy evidence of a child's performance, and capturing the essence of your instruction by their authenticity.

And contrary to many teachers' fears, most parents love portfolios! As she was looking at her daughter's portfolio for the first time during a parent-teacher conference, a parent in Bakersfield, California, said emphatically to a teacher, "Finally, I know what my daughter *can* do, not just what she *can't!*" After a teacher in Port Townsend, Washington, finished a conference, which included looking through the child's portfolio, the parent said, "This is the clearest conference I have ever had! I've never learned about such specifics before."

In our experience, when parents are informed about the purpose of the portfolio, they are the biggest supporters. In addition to the letter that has gone home previously (see Chapter 3), we send a letter with the portfolio the first time it goes home. In this letter we explain the contents of the portfolio and its role in the conference, and we provide directions for parents' written response.

A sample letter might look like this one (other examples appear in Appendix B):

Dear Parent,

　　Your child has worked hard for the past few months to develop his or her portfolio. He or she is bringing it home to share with you in a parent-child portfolio conference. Think of this selection as a story of your child's learning that he or she has chosen to tell. This may be a new experience for some of you, so I'd like to give you some tips:

- Let your child do most of the talking.
- Discuss why he or she chose the selections in the portfolio.
- Give only positive feedback.
- Do not make negative comments or criticisms.
- Ask your child what he or she can do now that is new.
- Talk about the child's goals.
- Enjoy your child's uniqueness.
- *Celebrate* your child's learning!

After the conference, write your child a note praising his or her learning and name his or her strengths as specifically as possible.

　　Please understand that children will treasure this note and will want to share it, so please take the time to compose it even if it's short. If you do not feel comfortable writing in English, feel free to use your own language. If you would like to tape your comments, we have tapes and tape recorders in the classroom. Ask your child to check one out.

The students have been very excited about sharing their portfolios with you. We are sure you will find the experience very meaningful. If you have any questions, please give me a call or stop by.

In responding to their child in writing after the conference, parents need to be told directly that negative comments, especially about messiness or invented spelling, are counterproductive. Letters should focus on positive aspects of the child's work, like this one to Lindsy (see also Appendix B):

Dear Lindsy,

This has been a wonderful project for the class. It has taught you how to analyze a work in depth, how to write critically about the work, and how to use your imagination to express thoughts suggested by the work.

I am very pleased with your portfolio, Lindsy. You devoted a lot of time to it and I believe that preparing it helped you learn a lot about the craft of writing. I think that your cleverness and sense of humor come through in your writing, which is facilitated by the tools you learned in this exercise.

Love,
Dad

◼︎▭ What about written follow-up?

Writing the assessment report is the last step in the portfolio process. More and more school districts are requiring that a short narrative accompany the report card. If you have used the components of assessment in this chapter, you have collected information that will help you write a narrative report about each student's growth in reading, writing, or the content areas. We follow a series of questions that guide the organization of our narrative report for each student (see Appendix A, form A.7).

A teacher narrative might look like this one:

Lisa, Grade 3
Language Arts Assessment

During this grading period the instruction in language arts revolved around reading and writing fairy tales. The work in Lisa's portfolio indicates that Lisa is able to read fairy tales and identify the unique elements of fairy tales. She uses these unique characteristics and weaves them into her writing of fairy tales as you can see from the fairy tales she included in her portfolio.

Lisa is beginning to use the strategies of mapping or outlining the main events of her story before she writes. She also used this strategy when she was comparing the fairy tale of Cinderella in the American and Chinese versions. She was able to determine similarities and differences. Lisa and I both set the goal to improve her ability to write comparison/contrast paragraphs.

Lisa shows progress in sharing her thoughts during the literature circles. She is able to support her ideas from the text and is taking more risks by putting forth her own ideas with her peers. She is able to identify and tell the significant elements in fairy tales and was able to find the common characteristics when comparing similar tales from different cultures.

Lisa was diligent in developing her portfolio and is beginning to write reflections of more insight. She is beginning to relate her learning to her life in a personal way. She finds it easier to clarify her goals and she seems to have a greater awareness when her reading strategies are not working. She is becoming quite resourceful in finding strategies that work.

■■■▭ How do we manage the record keeping?

You may want to include comments about a student's participation in the portfolio process on your assessment report, because it constitutes part of your language arts agenda. We want to emphasize, however, that the purpose of the report is not to assess the portfolio as an entity in itself; it is part of the self-assessment process.

It is our belief that students should manage as many aspects of their classroom operations as possible. Each student can be assigned a different record-keeping task and the responsibilities can rotate:

- monitor sign-up forms for peer conferences
- keep records of portfolios checked out to parents
- monitor sign-ups for teacher conferences
- maintain the portfolio storage box
- hand back papers for work folders
- account for the return of the portfolios to storage once they have gone home.

In some classrooms we've seen pocket charts that hold name cards for conference sign-ups. A student tracked the conferences on a form. Another student was responsible for tracking the portfolios that were ready to go home for parent conferences, and for checking them in when they were returned. If a portfolio was not returned to the classroom within five days, the student in charge sent a reminder to the parent. Two students kept the work folder box in order, and another two kept the storage box for the portfolios neat and orderly. (See Appendix A for forms and checklists that will help with record keeping.)

Since the portfolios are a source of great pride, they are often the first point of interest for guests who visit the classroom.

◼▭ What do portfolio containers look like?

Portfolios don't contain a whole year's work. They contain only the essence of a student's learning for that year. We find them most manageable when they contain only five to ten items at a time. This means that later items should replace earlier items as the portfolio continues to evolve throughout the year. Our worries about storage and managing paper were put to rest.

Portfolios are as varied as the students who create them and can be kept in a variety of containers, from an inexpensive manila folder to an expandable folder with a tie. Portfolios can also be kept in the large envelopes that hold bulky items like the students' bound books they make in class.

The important aspect of each portfolio is that it reflects the owner's uniqueness. Beth had the privilege of working with Pann Baltz (who was named the Walt Disney Teacher of the Year for 1993). Pann raided the supply room for 16-by-30-inch tagboard and designed portfolio folders for her students. She bound the folders with red bookbinding tape, and each student decorated his or her own.

In the early primary grades, some teachers have used 14-by-18-inch padded mailing envelopes to send the portfolio home. This packaging can hold the art projects, journals, student-bound books, cassette tapes and photos the kids or teachers have taken of special projects. Photographs can capture large projects that will not fit into an ordinary portfolio container.

Most teachers keep student portfolios in a box covered with contact paper or, if using file folders, in hanging files. Some store them in plastic milk carton boxes or plastic storage boxes with lids, both of which are available at discount stores. Portfolios are inexpensive and can be adapted to any school budget. Post-its and cassette tapes are more costly, but they can be purchased in bulk for much less. Reading cassettes need only be purchased for first graders—or at the grade level where teachers choose to begin using them. Once the cycle has started, the cassette moves with the student to the next grade. By the end of Grade 6, the tape should contain six years of reading and retelling assessments. Ask the PTA to help defray some of these costs, ask for donations from local corporations, and ask the students to write letters to members of the community.

We haven't forgotten to mention that some schools are moving in the direction of keeping portfolios on computers. This isn't a bad idea, but many schools are not yet technologically equipped to provide the number of computers this project requires. For more information on this topic, see Mathews (1990) and Hetterscheidt (1992).

◼▭ Summary

We have discussed peer conferences and teacher-student conferences. We addressed the portfolio process as it relates to students with special needs, the management of conferences, the role parents play in the portfolio process, the follow-up narrative to parents, and portfolio containers. We're finally ready to celebrate the students' achievements!

CHAPTER SIX

How Can We Celebrate Portfolios?

What does the process of building portfolios look like as a whole?

If we look back on the entire portfolio process, we have reason to celebrate! We have considered how to clarify the criteria, choose papers for the work folder, chart criteria, write self-reflections, hold conferences, prepare the portfolio itself, and share it.

Summary of the Portfolio Process

Weeks 1–9: Instruction and day-to-day assessment proceeds as usual with the added feature of clarifying criteria.
Weeks 1–3: Assignments are chosen for the work folder and the rest of the papers go home.

Weeks 4-6: Portfolio Charting begins and work is selected for the portfolio using the criteria on the chart. Self-assessment reflections are written and attached to the work.

Weeks 7-9: The portfolio is prepared by putting the work in order of priority and including a letter of introduction.

Weeks 8-9: Teachers and peers conduct conferences. Teacher writes narrative assessment reports.

Week 9: Parents conference with their child about the portfolio and write a letter. The portfolio is returned to school.

Portfolio Party!

What's left?

After parents have seen their child's portfolio and written their child a note, the portfolios should be returned to school. The end of a semester is a good time to celebrate their significance. Some teachers have a class party, and students share the most meaningful piece from their portfolio with the class. Others have a school portfolio party in the gym, the library, or the multipurpose room, and invite parents, grandparents, other relatives, and friends. Parent groups, like the PTA or parent volunteers, can be invited to help make the portfolio party a special occasion.

In one school, a mother single-handedly fired up a support group of parents and helped organize portfolio parties in every grade. She invited key members of the community and the local newspaper to celebrate what was positive about the local school. She said they could have skipped the decorations, balloons, and food because the kids were so involved in sharing their portfolios, they didn't even notice them.

Don't forget to make videotapes at the party that include student interviews about their accomplishments. Put the videos in the school library so that parents and kids can check them out and watch them at home. One teacher showed clips the following year at Back-to-School Night so parents would understand the process and the importance of portfolios in her classroom.

Picture this:

- a gym decorated with streamers and balloons
- a large banner on one wall that says "Portfolio Party"
- tables full of pizza, chips, cookies, punch, and Cokes
- chairs in groups around the gym
- students and their invited guests—parents, grandparents, aunts, uncles, friends—milling about impatiently, waiting for their portfolios to arrive

Believe it or not, no one is touching the food. Teachers finally enter with portfolios in hand. They are mobbed by their students, who are eager to share their portfolios with their guests. It gets late but no one moves toward the door. The room hums with animated discussions in every corner. The party was a success and everyone was thrilled!

Beyond the school site, the portfolio celebration is an excellent opportunity for public relations. All too often test scores make headlines, but they fail to convey what kids are really accomplishing every day in our classrooms. We propose that you send out a press release and extend a formal invitation to local newspapers, and radio and television stations. It's even more effective if students write the press releases (but make sure they're well edited). If the press does not show up, make sure a parent volunteer writes a story for the press that includes an interview with students. Using a videotaped segment is even more powerful. Isn't this good news?

What do we do with the portfolios when they return to school?

When portfolios are returned to school and the portfolio party is a happy memory, the portfolios should be stored in a box or file drawer in the classroom for easy access until the third or fourth week of the grading period. Then it is time to determine which new assignments and projects will reflect a learner's new knowledge. Some students may choose to take out many of the old items and replace them with new work during the new grading period, while others may want to keep pertinent work, like special projects, in the portfolio for the whole year. Remember that baseline data does not leave. Limit the number of pieces in the portfolio to from five to ten items. All other work must be taken home.

If students use spiral notebooks for reading and writing assignments, they can photocopy the work they want to designate as a portfolio possibility or attach a Post-it or marker that shows from the edge, and place the whole journal in the portfolio when it goes home. At other times the notebook is in daily use.

The portfolio goes back into its container until it is time for new portfolio selections, when the focus returns to work folders.

What do we do with the portfolio at the end of the school year?

The final portfolio of the school year can be called the Showcase or Master Portfolio. By the end of the school year the portfolio has changed as old items have been replaced by new work to indicate new learning, refinement of previous processes, or the achievement of new developmental stages. The material in the portfolio at the end of the school year should include selections the student has made to represent him or herself as a learner for that year, plus the first and last writing samples, the cassette tape containing one selection of the student's reading and retelling from the beginning and one from the end of the school year (and hard copies of the text). Other components of the assessment story may be added if the student wishes, such as the reading performance test and the rubric, or checklists, that show the teacher's assessment of growth and development for the whole year.

Teachers and administrators should decide whether the showcase portfolios are sent home, stored in the school, or continued from year to year. If the portfolio is allowed to go home, we suggest that the student bring the portfolio to school in the fall. Some schools actually send out letters requiring the return of the portfolio in the fall. This gives the portfolio status and purpose. Students have a vested interest in keeping their portfolio in good condition. The portfolio may or may not be part of the student's cumulative record.

Teachers may want to study students' portfolios sometime around the third or fourth week of the new school year. Each story of a student's growth from the previous school year is important baseline information for this year's instruction.

We are particularly excited about those schools that have students develop portfolios each year, kindergarten through twelfth grade, and then hand students their final showcase portfolio when they receive their diploma. This practice values each student's story of himself or herself as a learner. (If students move they should take their portfolios with them.)

The practice of using the portfolio for college entrance or for entry into the job market is becoming more commonplace. Teachers who are just entering the profession often create a portfolio to show school districts their range of expertise. If you'd like to find out more about these practices, see *Career Preparation Assessment: Portfolio Guidelines* (Far West Lab 1995), *Teacher Portfolios: Literacy Artifacts and Themes* (Rogers and Danielson 1997), and *Portfolios in Teacher Education* (McLaughlin and Vogt 1996).

Conclusion

Portfolios are powerful tools that refine teaching and learning. Teachers who are reluctant to try portfolios should take one step at a time. View the whole experience as a giant learning process that enables you to discern what you value as a teacher and use the feedback as a catalyst for improving your instruction and your understanding of how students learn.

The first year of portfolio development is a trial exploration that draws together many aspects of alternative assessment. Let the portfolio capture the juicy tidbits of learning that would otherwise travel home with students. We can almost guarantee that you will experience a philosophical transition and begin to want assessments that are more meaningful than letter grades.

Portfolios play an important role in this transition because they will give you the strategic information you need to make your evaluations and back your observations.

We wish you enjoyment!

Sample Forms

Reading and Listening Baseline Information

Name _____   Date _____
Grade _____   Teacher _____

Reading Section Level _____   Independent
                       _____   Instructional

Listening Level _____

Oral Reading Observations (Omit for Listening Selection)

_____ fluent
_____ knows some sight words
_____ uses phonics
_____ uses phonics exclusively
_____ uses context clues
_____ uses repetition

> **Key:**   + = excellent
>   ✓+ = very good
>   ✓ = good
>   ✓- = fair
>   - = poor

Retelling

_____ main points
_____ details
_____ in sequence

Comprehension

_____ main idea
_____ details
_____ vocabulary
_____ inference
_____ critical thinking

Strategies Observed

_____ uses background knowledge
_____ self-monitors and corrects
_____ synthesizes information
_____ makes meaningful substitutions

Strengths:

Areas in need of work:

Student's goals:

Teacher's goals:

- ESL—English as a Second Language
- Non-English Proficiency
- Limited English Proficiency

Student Reading Reflection Form

Name _____ **Date** _____
Grade _____ **Teacher** _____

Directions: Listen to the tape recording that we made yesterday and follow along with the text. Then answer the questions.

When I read the story, I _____

_____

_____

When I retold the story, I _____

_____

_____

I thought the questions were hard or easy because _____

_____

_____

My strengths in reading are _____

_____

_____

Words that I want to know are _____

_____

_____

Next, I'd like to get better at _____

_____

_____

Overall, I think that I _____

_____

_____

Writing Baseline Information

Name _____ Date _____ Grade _____
ESL _____ NEP _____ LEP _____ Teacher _____

Developmental Level _____ Drawing pictures
_____ Emergent writing
_____ Standard writing

Writing Observations

_____ dictates text
_____ writes in first language
_____ writes with invented spelling
_____ writes complete thoughts
_____ uses detail and descriptive language
_____ writes complex sentences
_____ writes for different audiences

Key:	+ = excellent
	✓+ = very good
	✓ = good
	✓- = fair
	– = poor

Organization

_____ uses prewriting strategies
_____ states a main idea
_____ story has beginning, middle, and end
_____ writes three related thoughts
_____ details support the main idea
_____ details in sequence

Process/Passion

_____ takes initiative for writing
_____ responds to teacher's questions
_____ has unique style, voice
_____ views self as writer

Mechanics

_____ uses punctuation correctly
_____ uses capitalization correctly
_____ uses standard grammar
_____ uses standard spelling

Strengths:

Areas in need of work:

Student's goals:

Teacher's goals:

- ESL—English as a Second Language
- Non-English Proficiency
- Limited English Proficiency

Content Area Baseline Information

Name _____ Date _____ Grade _____ Teacher _____
ESL_____ NEP_____ LEP_____ Content Area _____

Observations

_____ study habits
_____ interest in subject
_____ assignments completed
_____ participates in cooperative groups
_____ works independently
_____ participates in class discussions
_____ can read text
_____ has appropriate writing skills

> **Key:** + = excellent
> ✓+ = very good
> ✓ = good
> ✓- = fair
> - = poor

Skill Areas Needed for Competency

_____
_____
_____
_____
_____

Problem-Solving/Thinking Skills/Concepts in Subject Area

_____
_____
_____
_____
_____
_____

Strengths:

Areas in need of work:

Student's goals:

Teacher's goals:

- ESL—English as a Second Language
- Non-English Proficiency
- Limited English Proficiency

A.5

Peer Portfolio Conference Form

Name_____

Owner of the portfolio _____

Date _____

I am most impressed by _____

_____

_____

My favorite entry in the portfolio is _____

because _____ (name)

shows strengths in the following areas of reading or writing: _____

_____

_____

Recommendations I would make for next time_____

_____

_____

Additional comments:

Portfolio Conference Notes

Name _____

Subject/type of entry _____

Date _____

Student's reflections on:

Key:	+ = excellent
	✓+ = very good
	✓ = good
	✓- = fair
	- = poor

Criteria that were met:

Areas of growth:

Areas for development:

Teacher's reflections:

Areas of growth:

_____ eagerness to share portfolio

_____ organization of portfolio

_____ connecting to the criteria

_____ insight into learning

Student's goals:

Teacher's goals for the student:

Notes for Narrative Report

Student Name_____ **Date**_____

What strengths do I see?

What new strategies or processes do I see developing?

What progress or improvement can I track?

What goals does this student have and how can they be met?

What are my goals for this student and how can I meet these goals?

Peer Portfolio Conference Record

Name	Date/Initials	Comments

Parent Portfolio Conference Record

Name _____

Date Out	Date Returned	Date Out	Date Returned

Teacher Portfolio Conference Record

Name	Date/Initials	Comments

Sample Letters

Teachers' Letters to Parents

Dear Parents,

The children have been working so hard for Open House and they are very eager to show you all the results of their efforts. I am looking forward to seeing all of you tonight and know that it will be a very memorable experience for all of us.

A few weeks ago when the students had a pupil free day, the purpose was for the Camino Grove staff to be inserviced in a new and very exciting way of student assessment in California which is known as portfolio assessment. The most exciting aspect of this new approach is the way this involves students in looking at their own work. Children begin to assess and examine their own progress and begin to set exciting, realistic goals for themselves.

As you have observed at home, the students have been involved in looking at themselves as a person and as a learner through their work on personal paragraphs and their bio boxes. As a class, we brainstormed what we felt made a good writer. The list they came up with astonished me with its insight into the true heart of writing. Students have used this list, which you will see posted in out room tonight, to begin looking at their own work and identifying the assignments and projects which they feel best represent them as writers and as learners.

The students choose their work by placing sticky notes on it and writing down their reasons for selecting each item for their portfolio. This whole process is new to me, but I am very excited by what I see developing in the children. We are becoming more like partners in the learning process. My approach to teaching has always been to "jump in" even if the water looks a little deep. I have jumped into this portfolio process, believing in its value for your child's growth. However, this is the first open house in which I have given my students the freedom to select what they display, rather than giving them a set list of what to put in their folder.

You have a job when you come tonight. When you open your child's portfolio, you will find a note sheet on which I would like you to write your child a letter commenting on the positive growth and great things that you can see your child is learning. Try to be as specific as you can in your comments, and in this way, you will be modeling good writing skills for your child and affirming them at the same time.

Thank you for all your support this year and for your wonderful children. I'll look forward to seeing you tonight.

Sincerely,

Pann Baltz

Dear Parent,

   I am very excited to send home self-selected writing samples from your child's portfolio. We started off by discussing the elements of good writing. Then we looked at some student samples and developed a list of comments for good writing. Next, students worked with a buddy and chose from their writing portfolio three samples that they were proud of and that demonstrated how they'd grown as a writer since September. The students then made comments about the writing. We've also included a cassette tape of your child's reading.

   I hope you'll see the growth and progress your child has made! They all feel proud of their efforts and have identified how they can continue to grow as a reader/writer.

   Please read aloud and enjoy your child's portfolio and listen to the tape. Then write a letter to your child sharing your thoughts about what you enjoyed, noting the growth you see in your child's work.

   Please include your letter in the portfolio when you return it to school by:

_____.

   I'd also appreciate any comments you have!
   Sincerely,
   Karen Sekeres

Parent Letters to Students

Dear Ryan,

I know you are trying so hard to do your best this year. You have accomplished many goals. I am proud of you and will continue to support you in all that your do.

Love,
Mom

My dearest Diana,

WE ARE VERY PROUD OF THE GREAT JOB YOU HAVE DONE IN YOUR READING SKILLS SINCE ENTERING FIRST GRADE. WE HAVE LISTENED TO THE TAPE AND NOTED HOW MUCH YOU HAVE IMPROVED IN YOUR READING SKILLS. IT IS SO MUCH FUN TO SEE THE DIFFERENT READING STAGES OF LEARNING ABILITY. IT REMINDS US OF WHEN YOU WERE READY TO GIVE UP TRYING TO READ AND SAYING THAT YOU'LL NEVER BE ABLE TO READ. WELL, LISTENING TO THIS TAPE OF YOU READING ONLY REINFORCES THE FACT THAT YOU CAN DO OR LEARN ANYTHING YOU WANT TO IF YOU PUT YOUR MIND TO IT AND CONCENTRATE ON THAT SUBJECT AND ALSO NOT LET OTHER THINGS DISTRACT YOUR ATTENTION. MOM AND DAD ARE VERY PROUD OF YOU.

LOVE,
Mom and Dad

Parent Portfolio Feedback

The portfolio is very interesting. It has been a long time since I took Algebra I, so it is nice to again see the theory behind some of the concepts I still use today without thinking much about why they work.

I am pleased to see Marianne's mastery of the subject. She is obviously doing very well, despite an occasional struggle with the work. I see her doing her homework, so I feel good—and she should too—that she is getting good results from her work. And having a good teacher obviously helps both learning and keeping interest in the subject.

I am impressed with the neatness of her work, her systematic approach to study, and the fact that she got everything (or almost everything) correct. I have no specific suggestions at this time.

Signed,
Marianne's mom

Response to Portfolio Conference with Ernest's mother

The portfolio is very impressive. I am excited to see the great improvement Ernest has made in his writing: the style, the flow of the language, the use of descriptive words, the abilities to compare . . . etc. I had especially enjoyed reading the poem which is so very creative. I hope Ernest will keep up with his good work, and our sincerest thanks to Mrs. Ambler for her help and guidance.

Signed,

Ernest's mom

Bibliography

Anson, C. M., R. L. Brown, Jr., and L. Bridwell-Bowles. 1989. "Portfolio Assessment Across the Curriculum: Early Conflicts." In K. Greenburg and G. Slaughter, eds., *Notes from the National Testing Network in Writing.* Vol. 3 of a University of Minnesota document. Bloomington, IN: ERIC Clearinghouse on Reading and Communication Skills (ED 301 888).

Arter, J. A. 1990. Using Portfolios in Instruction and Assessment. Portland, OR: Northwest Regional Educational Laboratory. Report No. TM 016 096 (ERIC Document Reproduction Service No. ED 328 586).

Arter, J. A., and Vicki Spandel. 1992. *Using Portfolios of Student Work in Instruction and Assessment.* Portland, OR: Northwest Regional Educational Laboratory.

Atwell, Nancie. 1988. Making the Grade. In T. Newkirk and N. Atwell, eds., *Understanding Writing: Ways of Observing, Learning, and Teaching,* 2d ed., pp. 236–244. Portsmouth, NH: Heinemann.

Austin, Terri. 1994. *Changing the View: Student-Led Parent Conferences.* Portsmouth, NH: Heinemann.

Ballard, L. 1992. Portfolios and Self-assessment. *English Journal* 81, 2: 46–48.

Barrs, M. 1990. The Primary Language Record: Reflection of Issues in Evaluation. *Language Arts* 67: 244–253.

Barrs, M., and L. Laycock, eds. 1989. *Testing Reading.* London: Centre for Language in Primary Education.

Barrs, M., S. Ellis, H. Hester, and A. Thomas. 1988. *The Primary Language Record.* Portsmouth, NH: Heinemann.

———. 1990. *Patterns of Learning: The Primary Language Record and the National Curriculum.* London: Centre for Language in Primary Education.

Baskwill, J., and P. Whitman. 1988. *Evaluation: Whole Language, Whole Child.* New York: Scholastic.

Belanoff, P., and M. Dickson, eds. 1991. *Portfolios: Process and Product.* Portsmouth, NH: Heinemann–Boynton/Cook.

Bernhardt, Victoria L. 1994. A Framework for School Change—The School Portfolio (ERIC Document Reproduction Service No. ED 392168).

Bingham, A. 1988. Using Writing Folders to Document Student Progress. In T. Newkirk and N. Atwell, eds., *Understanding Writing: Ways of Observing, Learning, and Teaching,* 2d ed., pp. 216-225. Portsmouth, NH: Heinemann.

Bishop, W. 1989. Qualitative Evaluation and the Conversational Writing Classroom. *Journal of Teaching Writing* (special issue): 267-277.

Bracey, Gerald W. 1993. Assessing the New Assessments. *Principal* 72, 3: 34-36.

Brandt, R. 1987/1988. On Assessment in the Arts: A Conversation with Howard Gardner. *Educational Leadership* 45, 4: 30-34.

Broadfoot, P. 1988. Profiles and Records of Achievement: A Real Alternative. *Educational Psychology* 8, 4: 291-297.

Brown, N. 1987. Pivotal Pieces. *Portfolio* 1, 2: 9-13.

———. 1989. Portfolio Review: Pivots, Companions and Footprints. *Portfolio* 1, 4: 8-11.

Budnick, D., and S. Beaver. 1984. A Student Perspective on the Portfolio. *Nursing Outlook* 34, 5: 268-269.

Bunce-Crim, Marna. 1992. Evaluation: New Tools for New Tasks. *Instructor* 101, 7: 23-24, 26, 28-29.

Burnham, C. 1986. Portfolio Evaluation: Room to Breathe and Grow. In C. W. Bridges, ed., *Training the New Teacher of College Composition.* Bloomington, IN: ERIC Clearinghouse on Reading and Communication Skills (ED 264 589).

Burns, P., and B. D. Roe. 1993. *Burns/Roe Informal Reading Inventory.* Boston: Houghton Mifflin.

Caldwell, Natalie R., and Mary Ann Downs. 1995. The Gold Rush—A Fully Integrated Instructional Unit (ERIC Document Reproduction Service No. ED 389 198).

Calfee, R., and E. Hiebert. 1990. Classroom Assessment of Reading. In R. Barr et al., eds., *Handbook of Reading Research.* Vol. 2. White Plains, NY: Longman.

Calfee, R. C. 1987. The School as a Context for Assessment of Literacy. *Reading Teacher* 40, 8: 738-743.

Calfee, Robert C., and Pam Perfumo. 1993. Student Portfolios: Opportunities for a Revolution in Assessment. *Journal of Reading* 36, 7: 532-537.

Calkins, Lucy McCormick. 1991. *Living Between the Lines.* Portsmouth, NH: Heinemann.

Camp, R. 1990. Thinking Together About Portfolios. *Quarterly* 12, 2: 8-14, 27.

Campbell, Jo. 1992. Laser Disk Portfolios: Total Child Assessment. *Educational Leadership* 49, 8: 69-70.

Career Preparation Assessment. Portfolio Guidelines. 1995. San Francisco: Far West Lab for Educational Research and Development.

Carr, B. 1987. Portfolios. *School Arts* 86: 55-66.

Carter, M., and R. J. Tierney. 1988. Reading and Writing Growth: Using Portfolios in Assessment. Paper presented at National Reading Conference, Tucson, AZ, May.

Chapman, C. 1990. Authentic Writing Assessment. Washington, DC: American Institutes for Research, Report No. EDO-TM-90-4 (ERIC Document Reproduction Service No. ED 328 606).

Clay, Marie. 1979. *The Early Detection of Reading Difficulties,* 3d ed. Portsmouth, NH: Heinemann.

———. 1990. Research Currents: What Is and What Might Be in Evaluation. *Language Arts* 67, 3: 288–298.

———. 1991. *Reading Recovery: A Guidebook for Teachers in Training.* Portsmouth, NH: Heinemann.

———. 1993. *An Observation Survey of Early Literacy Achievement.* Portsmouth, NH: Heinemann.

Clemmons, Joan. 1991. Engaging the Learner in Whole Literacy: An Immersion Approach. Workshop presented at the Annual Meeting of the International Reading Association, Las Vegas, NV, May.

Clemmons, J., et al. 1993. *Portfolios in the Classroom: A Teacher's Sourcebook.* New York: Scholastic.

Collins, A. 1990. Portfolios for Assessing Student Learning in Science: A New Name for a Familiar Idea? In A. B. Champagne, B. E. Lovitts, and B. E. Callinger, eds., *Assessment in the Service of Instruction.* Washington, DC: American Association for the Advancement of Science.

Cooper, C. R. 1977. Holistic Evaluation of Writing. In C. R. Cooper and L. Odell, eds., *Evaluating Writing: Describing, Measuring, Judging.* Urbana, IL: National Council of Teachers of English.

Cooper, W., and B. J. Brown. 1992. Using Portfolios to Empower Student Writers. *English Journal* 81, 2: 40–45.

Cooper, W., and J. Davies, eds. 1990. *Portfolio News.* Encinitas, CA: Portfolio Assessment Clearing House.

Cortez, Suzanne E. 1994. The Challenge of Reform: How Are Kentucky Teachers Changing Their Roles and Perceptions? Paper Presented at the Annual Meeting of the Mid-South Educational Research Association, Nashville, TN, November.

DeFina, Allan A. 1992. *Portfolio Assessment: Getting Started.* New York: Scholastic.

De Fina, A. A., L. L. Anstendig, and K. De Lawter. 1991. Alternative Integrated Reading/Writing Assessment and Curriculum Design. *Journal of Reading* 34, 5: 354–359.

Degavarian, D. A. 1989. Portfolio Assessment. Bloomington, IN: ERIC Clearinghouse on Reading and Communication Skills (ED 306 894).

Edelsky, C., B. Altwerger, and B. Flores. 1991. *Whole Language: What's the Difference?* Portsmouth, NH: Heinemann.

Educational Testing Service. 1989. *The Student Writer: An Endangered Species?* Focus 23. Princeton, NJ: Education Testing Service.

Elbow, P., and P. Belanoff. 1986. Portfolios as a Substitute for Proficiency Examinations. *College Composition and Communication* 37, 3: 336–339.

Farr, R., and R. F. Carey. 1986. *Reading: What Can Be Measured?* 2d ed. Newark, DE: International Reading Association.

Farr, R., et al. 1990. Writing in Response to Reading. *Educational Leadership* 47, 6: 66-69.

Farr, R., and K. Lowe. 1990. Alternative Assessment in Language Arts. Paper presented at the National Symposium on Alternative Assessment, Indiana University, Bloomington, IN.

Farr, Roger, and Bruce Tone. 1994. *Portfolio Performance Assessment: Helping Students Evaluate Their Progress as Readers and Writers.* Fort Worth, TX: Harcourt Brace.

Ferguson, Shelley, and Carole Maples. 1992. Windows on Learning. Portfolios Part II: Zeroing in on Math Abilities. *Learning* 21, 3: 38-41.

Fiderer, A., et al. 1991. *A Language Arts Portfolio Handbook: Alternative Assessment Strategies for K-5 Teachers.* (Available from Scarsdale Public School System, Scarsdale, NY.)

Flood, J., and D. Lapp. 1989. Reporting Reading Progress: A Comparison Portfolio for Parents. *Reading Teacher* 42, 7: 508-514.

Floden, Robert E., et al. 1995. Capacity Building in Systemic Reform. *Phi Delta Kappa* 77, 1: 19-21.

Fontana, Jean. 1995. Portfolio Assessment: Its Beginnings in Vermont and Kentucky. *NASSP Bulletin* 79, 573: 25-30.

Ford, J. E., and G. Larkin. 1978. The Portfolio System: An End to Backsliding Writing Standards. *College English* 39, 8: 950-955.

Frazier, Darlene M., and Leon F. Paulson. 1992. How Portfolios Motivate Reluctant Writers. *Educational Leadership* 49, 8: 62-65.

Fredericks, A. D., and T. V. Rasinski. 1990a. Involving Parents in the Assessment Process. *Reading Teacher* 44, 4: 346-349.

———. 1990b. Whole Language and Parents: Natural Partners. *Reading Teacher* 43, 9: 692-693.

Frederiksen, J. R., and A. Collins. 1989. A Systems Approach to Educational Testing. *Educational Researcher* 18, 9: 27-32.

Gable, R. A., J. M. Hendrickson, and J. W. Meeks. 1988. Assessing Spelling Errors of Special Needs Students. *Reading Teacher* 42, 2: 112-117.

Galleher, D. 1987. Assessment in Context: Toward a National Writing Project Model. *Quarterly* 9, 3: 5-7.

Gearhart, Maryl. 1992. *Writing Portfolios at the Elementary Level: A Study of Methods for Writing Assessment.* Los Angeles: Center for Research on Evaluation, Standards, and Student Testing.

Gee, J. P. 1988. Discourse Systems and Aspirin Bottles: On Literacy. *Journal of Education* 170, 1: 27-40.

Gilmore, P. 1991. "'Gimme Room': School Resistance, Attitude, and Access to Literacy." In C. Mitchell and K. Weiler, eds., *Rewriting Literacy: Culture and the Discourse of the Other,* pp. 57-73. New York: Bergin and Garvey.

Glazer, Susan Mandel, and Carol Smullen Brown. 1993. *Portfolios and Beyond: Collaborative Assessment in Reading and Writing.* Norwood, MA: Christopher-Gordon.

Goins, Brad. 1992. ERIC/EECE Report: Reporting to Parents. *Childhood Education* 69, 1: 56-57.

Goldberg, M. F. 1992. Portrait of Shirley Brice Heath. *Educational Leadership* 49, 7: 80-82.

Gomez, M. L., M. E. Graue, and M. N. Bloch. 1991. Reassessing Portfolio Assessment: Rhetoric and Reality. *Language Arts* 68, 8: 620-628.

Goodman, K. 1986. *What's Whole in Whole Language?* Portsmouth, NH: Heinemann.

Goodman, K., Y. Goodman, and W. Hood. 1988. *The Whole Language Evaluation Book.* Portsmouth, NH: Heinemann.

Goodman, Y., D. Watson, and C. Burke. 1987. *Reading Miscue Inventory: Alternate Procedures.* Katanah, NY: Richard C. Owen.

Gottlieb, Margo. 1995. Nurturing Student Learning Through Portfolios. *TESOL Journal* 5, 1: 12–14.

Grace, C., and E. Shore. 1991. *The Portfolio and Its Use: Developmentally Appropriate Assessment of Young Children.* Little Rock, AR: Southern Association on Children Under Six.

Grady, E. 1992. *The Portfolio Approach to Assessment.* Bloomington, IN: Phi Delta Kappa Educational Foundation.

Graves, Donald H., and Bonnie S. Sunstein. 1992. *Portfolio Portraits.* Portsmouth, NH: Heinemann.

Hackmann, Donald G., et al. 1995. Student-Led Conferences: Encouraging Student-Parent Academic Discussions. Paper presented at the Annual Conference of the National Middle School Association, New Orleans, November.

Hannam, Susan E. 1995. Portfolios: An Alternative Method of Student and Program Assessment. *Journal of Athletic Training* 30, 4: 338–341.

Hansen, J. 1987. *When Writers Read.* Portsmouth, NH: Heinemann.

———. 1992a. Literacy Portfolios: Helping Students Know Themselves. *Educational Leadership* 49, 8: 66–68.

———. 1992b. Literacy Portfolios Emerge. *Reading Teacher* 45, 8: 604–607.

———. 1992c. Students' Evaluations Bring Reading and Writing Together. *Reading Teacher* 46, 2: 100–105.

Harnack, Andrew, et al. 1994. The Impact of Kentucky's Educational Reform Act on Writing Throughout the Commonwealth. *Composition Chronicle: Newsletter for Writing Teachers* 7, 8: 4–7.

Harp, Bill. 1991. *Assessment and Evaluation in Whole Language Programs.* Norwood, MA: Christopher-Gordon.

Harris, K. 1992. Resource Room Students Set Their Own Goals. Paper presented at the meeting of the New England Reading Association, Manchester, NH, November.

———. 1993. "Interviews to Supplement Tests." In Researchers Reflect: Writings from the Manchester Portfolio Project, 1990–92. Durham, NH: University of New Hampshire, Writing Lab.

Hashem, Mahoub E. 1995. Assessing Student Learning Outcomes in Teaching Intercultural Communication. Paper presented at the Annual Meeting of the Speech Communication Association, San Antonio, November.

Hebert, Elizabeth A. 1992. Portfolios Invite Reflection—From Students and Staff. *Educational Leadership* 49, 8: 58–61.

Hebert, Elizabeth A., and Laurie Schultz. 1996. The Power of Portfolios. *Educational Leadership* 53, 7: 70–71.

Herter, R. J. 1991. Writing Portfolios: Alternatives to Testing. *English Journal* 80, 1: 90–91.

Hetterscheidt, Judy. 1992. Using the Computer as a Reading Portfolio. *Educational Leadership* 49, 8: 73.

Hewitt, Geof. 1995. *A Portfolio Primer: Teaching, Collecting, and Assessing Student Writing.* Portsmouth, NH: Heinemann.

Hill, Bonnie Campbell, and Cynthia Ruptic. 1994. *Practical Aspects of Authentic Assessment: Putting the Pieces Together.* Norwood, MA: Christopher-Gordon.

Howard, K. 1990. Making the Writing Portfolio Real. *Quarterly of the National Writing Project and the Center for the Study of Writing* 12, 2: 4-7, 27.

Huffman, Priscilla D. 1996. "Look What I Did": Why Portfolio-Based Assessment Works. *Early Childhood News* 8, 1: 20-23.

Hunt, D. C. 1986. Preparing a Portfolio. *Instrumentalist* 41: 30-38.

Jardine, Antoinette S. 1996. Key Points of the "Authentic" Assessment Portfolio. *Intervention in School and Clinic* 31, 4: 252-253.

Jasmine, J. 1992. *Portfolio Assessment for Your Whole Language Classroom.* Huntington Beach, CA: Teacher Created Materials.

Jenkins, Carol Brennan. 1996. *Inside the Writing: What We Need to Know to Assess Children's Writing.* Portsmouth, NH: Heinemann.

Jett-Simpson, M., et al. 1990. *Toward an Ecological Assessment of Reading.* Madison, WI: Wisconsin State Reading Association.

Johns, J. L. 1990. Literacy Portfolios. DeKalb, IL: Northern Illinois University, Reading Clinic. Report No. CS 010 074 (ERIC Document Reproduction Service No. ED 319 020).

Johnsma, K. S. 1989. Questions and Answers: Portfolio Assessment. *Reading Teacher* 43, 4: 264-265.

Johnston, P. 1984. Assessment in Reading. In P. D. Pearson et al., eds., *Handbook of Research in Reading.* Vol. 1. White Plains, NY: Longman.

———. 1987a. *Assessing the Process, and the Process of Assessment in the Language Arts: The Dynamics of Language Learning.* Urbana, IL: National Council of Teachers of English.

———. 1987b. Teachers as Evaluation Experts. *Reading Teacher* 40, 8: 744-748.

———. 1989. "Steps Toward a More Naturalistic Approach to the Assessment of the Reading Process." In J. Algina and S. Legg, eds., *Cognitive Assessment of Language and Mathematics Outcomes.* Norwood, NJ: Ablex.

Jongsma, K. S. 1989. Portfolio Assessment. *Reading Teacher* 43, 3: 264-265.

Jordan, R. Rosalie. 1992. Literacy Assessment Forum. *In the Eye of the Storm* 1, 3: 12-14.

Kohn, Alfie. 1993. *Punished by Rewards: The Trouble with Gold Stars, Incentive Plans, A's, Praise, and Other Bribes.* Boston: Houghton Mifflin.

———. 1996. *Beyond Discipline: From Compliance to Community.* Alexandria, VA: Association for Supervision and Curriculum Development.

Koretz, Daniel. 1994. The Evolution of a Portfolio Program: The Impact and Quality of the Vermont Portfolio Program in Its Second Year (1992-93). Los Angeles: National Center for Research and Evaluation, Standards, and Student Testing.

Krest, M. 1987. Time on My Hands: Handling the Paper Load. *English Journal* 76, 8: 37-42.

———. 1990. Adapting the Portfolio to Meet Student Needs. *English Journal* 79, 2: 29-34.

Kurtz, Kevin. 1996. It's in the Box. *Executive Educator* 18, 2: 30-31.

Lamme, L. L., and C. Hysmith. 1991. One School's Adventure into Portfolio Assessment. *Language Arts* 68, 8: 629-640.

Le Countryman, Lyn, and Merrie Schroeder. 1996. When Students Lead Parent-Teacher Conferences. *Educational Leadership* 53, 7: 64–68.

Lee, Elizabeth A. 1992. Reflecting on Teaching. Paper presented at the Annual Meeting of the American Educational Research Association, San Francisco, April.

Levi, R. 1990. Assessment and Educational Vision: Engaging Learners and Parents. *Language Arts* 67, 3: 269–273.

Lipa, S. E., R. P. Harlin, and S. Phelps. 1991. Portfolio Assessment: Diagnostic Implications. Paper presented at the meeting of the National Reading Conference, Palm Springs, CA, December.

Los Alimitos [California] Unified School District. 1990. Samples of language arts portfolio, grades K–12. Typescript.

Louie, A. 1982. *Yeh Shen: A Cinderella Story from China.* New York: Sandcastle Books.

Lucas, C. K. 1988a. Toward Ecological Evaluation, Part 1. *Quarterly* 10, 1: 1–3, 12–17.

———. 1988b. Toward Ecological Evaluation, Part 2. *Quarterly,* 10, 2: 4–10.

Mathews, J. 1990. From Computer Management to Portfolio Assessment. *Reading Teacher* 43, 6: 420–421.

McLaughlin, Maureen, and MaryEllen Vogt. 1996. *Portfolios in Teacher Education.* Newark, DE: International Reading Association.

McKenna, M. C., and D. J. Kear. 1990. Measuring Attitude Toward Reading: A New Tool for Teachers. *Reading Teacher* 43, 9: 626–639.

McNeil, John D. 1987. *Reading Comprehension: New Directions for Classroom Practice.* Glenview, IL: Scott, Foresman.

Moening, Amy A., and Navaz Peshotan Bhavnagri. 1996. *Early Education and Development* 7, 2: 179–199.

Ohanian, Susan. 1992. Energize Your Math Program! *Instructor* 101, 8: 44–46, 48–49.

O'Neil, John. 1993. The Promise of Portfolios. *Update* 35, 7.

Paterson, Katherine. 1987. *Bridge to Terabithia.* New York: HarperCollins.

Partridge, S. 1990. Assessing Students' Writing in the 1990s: A Discussion. Report No. CS 212. 462 (ERIC Document Reproduction Service No. ED 322 512).

Paulson, F. L., and P. R. Paulson. How Do Portfolios Measure Up? A Cognitive Model for Assessing Portfolios. Union, WA: Northwest Evaluation Association. Report No. TM 015 516 (ERIC Document Reproduction Service No. ED 324 329).

Paulson, F. L., P. R. Paulson, and C. A. Meyer. 1991. What Makes a Portfolio a Portfolio? *Educational Leadership* 48, 5: 60–63.

Paulson, P. R., and F. L. Paulson. 1991. Portfolios: Stories of Knowing. In P. H. Dreyer, ed., *Claremont Reading Conference 55th Yearbook 1991. Knowing: The Power of Stories,* pp. 294–303. Claremont, CA: Center for Developmental Studies, Claremont Graduate School.

Pearson, P. D., and S. Valencia. 1987. Assessment, Accountability and Professional Prerogative. In J. E. Readence and R. S. Baldwin, eds., *Research in Literacy: Merging Perspectives.* Thirty-sixth yearbook of the National Reading Conference. Rochester, NY: National Reading Conference.

Pearson, P. D., L. R. Roehler, J. Dole, and G. G. Duffy. 1992. Developing Expertise in Reading Comprehension. In S. J. Samuels and A. E. Farstrup, eds., *What Research Has to Say About Reading Instruction.* Newark, DE: International Reading Association.

Peters, C. W. 1991. You Can't Have Authentic Assessment Without Authentic Content. *Reading Teacher* 44, 8: 590–591.

Pikulski, J. J. 1989. The Assessment of Reading: A Time for Change? *Reading Teacher* 43, 1: 80–81.

The Primary Program: Report from the Task Force on Improving Kentucky Schools. 1995. Lexington, KY: Prichard Committee for Academic Excellence (ERIC Document Reproduction Service No. ED 389 399).

Probst, R. 1988. *Response and Analysis: Teaching Literature in Junior and Senior High School.* Portsmouth, NH: Heinemann.

Purves, A. C. 1992. Reflections on Research and Assessment in Written Composition. *Research in the Teaching of English* 26, 1: 108–122.

Raines, Peggy. 1996. Writing Portfolios: Turning the House into a Home. *English Journal* 85, 1: 41–45.

Rayer, J. K. 1991. *Portfolio Assessment for Early Childhood Educators.* (Available from Mainz American Elementary School, Box 524 HHC-USMCA, APO New York, NY 09185.)

Rhodes, L. K., and S. Nathenson-Mejia. 1992. Anecdotal Records: A Powerful Tool for Ongoing Literacy Assessment. *Reading Teacher* 45, 7: 502–509.

Rief, L. 1990. Finding the Value in Evaluation: Self-Assessment in a Middle School Classroom. *Educational Leadership* 47, 6: 24–29.

———. 1992. *Seeking Diversity: Language Arts with Adolescents.* Portsmouth, NH: Heinemann.

Rogers, Sheri Everts, and Kathy Everts Danielson. 1997. *Teacher Portfolios: Literacy Artifacts and Themes.* Portsmouth, NH: Heinemann.

Rousculp, E. E., and G. H. Maring. 1992. Portfolios for a Community of Learners. *Journal of Reading* 35, 5: 378–385.

Routman, R. 1988. *Transitions: From Literature to Literacy.* Portsmouth, NH: Heinemann.

———. 1991. *Invitations: Changing as Teacher and Learners, K-12.* Portsmouth, NH: Heinemann.

Rynkofs, J. T. 1988. Send Your Writing Folders Home. In T. Newkirk and N. Atwell, eds., *Understanding Writing: Ways of Observing, Learning, and Teaching,* 2d ed., pp. 236–224. Portsmouth, NH: Heinemann.

Santa, Carol M. 1995. Assessment: Students Lead Their Own Parent Conferences. *Teaching Pre K-8* 25, 7: 92–94.

Scardamalia, M., and C. Bereiter. 1983. Child as Coinvestigator: Helping Children Gain Insight into Their Own Mental Processes. In S. G. Paris, G. M. Olson, and H. W. Stevenson, eds., *Learning and Motivation in the Classroom,* pp. 61–82. Hillsdale, NJ: Lawrence Erlbaum.

———. 1985. Fostering the Development of Self-Regulation in Children's Knowledge Processing. In S. S. Chipman, J. W. Segal, and R. Glaser, eds., *Thinking and Learning Skills. Vol. 2: Research and Open Questions,* pp. 563–578. Hillsdale, NJ: Lawrence Erlbaum.

Seigel, S. 1989. Even Before Portfolios: The Activities and Atmosphere of a Portfolio Classroom. *Portfolio* 1, 5: 6–9.

Shakelford, Ray L. 1996. Student Portfolios: A Process/Product Learning and Assessment Strategy. *Technology Teacher* 55, 8: 31–36.

Sharp, Q. Q. 1989. *Evaluation: Whole Language Checklists for Evaluating Your Children for Grades K to 6*. New York: Scholastic.

Shepard, L. A. 1989. Why We Need Better Assessments. *Educational Leadership* 46, 7: 4-9.

Simmons, J. 1990. Portfolios as Large-Scale Assessment. *Language Arts* 67, 3: 262-267.

———. 1991. Large-Scale Portfolio Evaluation of Writing. Ph.D. diss., University of New Hampshire, Durham.

Smolen, Lynn, et al. 1995. Developing Student Self-Assessment Strategies. *TESOL Journal* 5, 1: 22-27.

Smith, Robert Kimmel. 1972. *Chocolate Fever.* New York: Putnam/Dell.

Spandel, V., and R. J. Stiggins. 1990. *Creating Writers: Linking Assessment and Writing Instruction.* White Plains, NY: Longman.

Stayter, F. Z., and P. Johnston. 1990. Evaluating the Teaching and Learning of Literacy. In T. Shanahan, ed., *Reading and Writing Together: New Perspectives for the Classroom,* pp. 253-271. Norwood, MA: Christopher-Gordon.

Stewart, Roger A. 1993. Portfolios: Agents of Change (Have You Read?). *Reading Teacher* 46, 6: 522-524.

Sucher, F., and R. A. Allred. 1981. *The New Sucher-Allred Reading Placement Inventory.* Oklahoma City, OK: Economy.

Taylor, D. 1990. Teaching Without Testing. *English Education* 22, 1: 4-74.

Tierney, Robert J. 1992. Portfolios: Windows on Learning. Setting a New Agenda for Assessment, *Learning* 21, 2: 61-64.

Tierney, Robert J., Mark A. Carter, and Laura E. Desai. 1991. *Portfolio Assessment in the Reading-Writing Classroom.* Norwood, MA: Christopher-Gordon.

Valencia, S. 1990. A Portfolio Approach to Classroom Reading Assessment: The Whys, Whats, and Hows. *Reading Teacher* 43, 4: 338-340.

Valencia, S. W., E. H. Hiebert, and P. P. Afflerbach. 1994. *Authentic Reading Assessment: Practices and Possibilities.* Newark, DE: International Reading Association.

Valencia, S., W. McGinley, and P. D. Pearson. 1990a. Assessing Reading and Writing: Building a More Complete Picture for Middle School Assessment. Champaign, IL: University of Illinois, Center for the Study of Reading. Report No. CS 010 116 (ERIC Document Reproduction Service No. ED 320 121).

———. 1990b. Assessing Reading and Writing. In G. Duffy, ed., *Reading in the Middle School,* pp. 124-153. Newark, DE: International Reading Association.

Valencia, S., and P. D. Pearson. 1987. Reading Assessment: Time for a Change. *Reading Teacher* 40, 8: 726-732.

———. 1990. National Survey of the Use of Test Data for Educational Decision-Making. Reading Research and Education Center Technical Report, Champaign IL: University of Illinois.

Vavrus, L. G. 1990. Put Portfolios to the Test. *Instructor* 100, 1: 48-53.

Vavrus, L. G., et al. 1988. *Portfolio Development Handbook for Teachers of Elementary Literacy.* Technical Report L05. Teacher Assessment Project, Stanford University.

Vermont Department of Education. 1989. *Vermont Writing Assessment: The Portfolio.* Montpelier, VT: Vermont Department of Education.

Weaver, C. 1988. *Reading Process and Practice from Socio-psycholinguistics to Whole Language.* Portsmouth, NH: Heinemann.

Werner, Patrice H. 1992. Integrated Assessment System. *Journal of Reading* 35, 5: 416-418.

White, E. 1985. *Teaching and Assessing Writing.* San Francisco: Jossey-Bass.

Whittier, S. A. 1989. Portfolio Reflections: Personalizing Education with Portfolios. *Portfolio* 1, 4: 5-7.

Wiggins, G. 1989. Teaching to the (Authentic) Test. *Educational Leadership* 46, 7: 41-47.

Winner, E., and E. Rosenblatt. 1989. Tracking the Effects of the Portfolio Process: What Changes and When? *Portfolio* 1, 5: 21-26.

Winograd, P., S. Paris, and C. Bridge. 1991. Improving the Assessment of Literacy. *Reading Teacher* 45, 2: 108-116.

Wolf, D. P. 1987/1988. Opening up Assessment. *Educational Leadership* 45, 4: 24-29.

———. 1989. Portfolio Assessment: Sampling Student Work. *Educational Leadership* 46, 7: 35-39.

Wolf, K. P., S. Athanases, and E. Chin. 1988. Designing Portfolios for the Assessment of Elementary Literacy Teaching: Work-in-Progress. Stanford, CA: Stanford University, Teacher Assessment Project, School of Education. Report No. CS 009 495 (ERIC Document Reproduction Service No. ED 302 842).

Yancey, K. B., ed. 1992. *Portfolios in the Writing Classroom: An Introduction.* Urbana, IL: National Council of Teachers of English.

Zessoules, R. 1989. The Dance Marathon: Learning Over Time. *Portfolio* 1, 5: 11-19.

———. 1990a. Adapting Portfolios for Large-Scale Use. *Educational Leadership* 47, 6: 28.

———. 1990b. Portfolios as Large-Scale Assessment. *Language Arts* 67: 262-268.

5161